Quit the Nigh. ... ... Day!

This book is designed for the reader interested in ritual magic and the deeper significant principles of the magic of the Golden Dawn, possibly the most famous hermetic order the world has known. The author takes you through the steps of applying to join a temple and tells you what goes on behind the scenes if your application is accepted or rejected.

The first steps into the grade of Neophyte are shown as well as how and why the ritualistic process unfolds during this initiatory ritual. The author describes some first-hand experiences of those who have undergone this ritual, tells you what to expect, and provides study guidelines to go with it. This book shows what happens through the eyes of an initiate of possibly the best-known occult system in the world today.

In the past, there have been books about the Golden Dawn, but, with the exception of those by Israel Regardie, these have not been written by initiates of any legitimate temple. Pat Zalewski takes you deep into the hidden mysteries of the Golden Dawn from the viewpoint of one of its highest initiates. For those who want to study magic in a group ritual format, this book takes you through the processes of hermetic ritual with firm guidelines and dos and don'ts. This book was written to help those in existing Golden Dawn temples explain the previously unpublished teachings of the Order. For individuals who wish to utilize magic in the privacy of their own homes, this book is a must, for it teaches you about magic as well as the traps and about shortcuts that can be applied on a solo basis.

This book is the first of a series on the grade rituals of the Golden Dawn and covers the initiation ceremony for the Neophyte grade. In the past, the ritual and explanations from Order papers have been published, but Zalewski gives much more. He gives not only the official explanations but also a great deal of additional information, all blended together into a complete new lecture, which he has entitled Z-5. There are completely new dimensions to ritual work in this book. It is a must for all those who wish to practice the light-seeking, self-realizing magic of the Golden Dawn.

About the Author

Patrick Zalewski is a 7=4 Adept of the Golden Dawn and co-chief with his wife, Chris, of the Thoth-Hermes Temple in New Zealand. He has at his disposal material from the Whare Ra Temple of the Stella Matutina which has never before been seen in print. He is a practicing magician rather than one of the armchair variety who merely theorizes about magic. Pat and Chris have spent the last ten years in dedicated research, preservation, and development of the Golden Dawn material placed in their care by the Adepts of Whare Ra. They are writing a number of books which detail their experiences with the Golden Dawn.

To Write to the Author

We cannot guarantee that every letter written to the author can be answered, but all will be forwarded. Both the author and the publisher appreciate hearing from readers, learning of your enjoyment and benefit from this book. Llewellyn also publishes a bi-monthly news magazine with news and reviews of practical esoteric studies and articles helpful to the student, and some readers' questions and comments to the author may be answered through this magazine's columns if permission to do so is included in the original letter. The author sometimes participates in seminars and workshops, and dates and places are announced in *The Llewellyn New Times*. For more information about the Golden Dawn or to ask a question, write to:

Ra-Horakhty Temple, Hermetic Society of the Golden Dawn
31849 Pacific Highway South, Suite 107
Federal Way, Washington 98003

To write to the author, write to:

Pat Zalewski
c/o THE LLEWELLYN NEW TIMES
P.O. Box 64383-897, St. Paul, MN 55164-0383, U.S.A.
Please enclose a self-addressed, stamped envelope for reply, or $1.00 to cover costs.

LLEWELLYN'S GOLDEN DAWN SERIES

Z-5
Secret Teachings of the Golden Dawn

Book I
The Neophyte Ritual
0=0

by

Pat Zalewski

1991
Llewellyn Publications
St. Paul, Minnesota 55164–0383, U.S.A.

FIRST EDITION

Illustrations by Richard Dudschus and David Stoelk
Photography by Nikolaj C. Bell

Library of Congress Cataloging-in-Publication Data
Zalewski, Pat, 1948-
    Z-5 : secret teachings of the Golden Dawn / Pat Zalewski. — 1st ed.
      p. cm. — (Llewellyn's Golden Dawn series)
    Contents: Bk. 1. The neophyte ritual, 0=0
    ISBN 0–87542–897–5 (v. 1) : $12.95
    1. Hermetic Order of the Golden Dawn—Rituals. I. Title.
    II. Title: Z five. III. Series.
BF1623.R7Z34 1991
135'.4—dc20   90-26728
                                                CIP

Llewellyn Publications
A Division of Llewellyn Worldwide, Ltd.
P.O. Box 64383, St. Paul, MN 55164-0383

ABOUT LLEWELLYN'S GOLDEN DAWN SERIES

Just as, 100 years ago, the original Order of the Golden Dawn *initiated* a powerful rebirth of interest in The Western Esoteric Tradition that has lasted through this day, so do we expect this series of books of add new impetus to The Great Work itself among an ever broadening base of sincere students.

> *I further promise and swear that with the Divine Permission, I will from this day forward, apply myself to the Great Work—which is: to purify and exalt my Spiritual Nature so that with the Divine Aid I may at length attain to be more than human, and thus gradually raise and unite myself to my Higher and Divine Genius, and that in this event I will not abuse the great power entrusted to me.*

With this oath, the *Adeptus Minor* of the Inner Order committed him/herself to undertake, consciously and deliberately, that which was ordained as the birthright of all Humanity: TO BECOME MORE THAN HUMAN!

It is this that is the ultimate message of Esotericism: that evolution continues, and that the purpose of each life is to grow into the Image set for us by our Creator: to attain and reveal our own Divinity.

These books and tapes will themselves make more easily accessible the Spiritual Technology that is inherent in the Golden Dawn System. It is a system that allows for individual as well as group endeavor; a system that works within or without an organized lodge; a system that is based on universal principles that will be shown to be global in their impact today.

And it is practical. The works in this series will be practical in their application. You need neither travel to the Mountain Top nor obtain any tool other than your own Consciousness. No garment need you other than that of your own Imagination. No authority need you other than that of your own True Will.

Set forth, then, into The New Dawn—a New Start on the greatest adventure there is: to become One with the Divine Genius.

Other Books by Pat Zalewski

The Secret Inner Order Rituals of the Golden Dawn
(Falcon Press, 1988)

Golden Dawn Enochian Magic
(Llewellyn Publications, 1990)

Forthcoming from Llewellyn

Equinox and Solstice Rituals of the Golden Dawn

Z-5 Secret Teachings of the Golden Dawn
Book II: The Zelator Ritual 1=10

The Kabbalah of the Golden Dawn

Dedication

To Laura Jennings-Yorke, a friend and adept

Contents

Foreword

With the publication of this volume, Llewellyn Publications begins a new era of Golden Dawn history and magical practice. Whether the student is a member of a group, a temple, or a solitary practitioner, he/she will be able to use this information to enrich his/her magical practice.

The 0=0 Commentary is the first of five books which will explain in depth the Neophyte and Elemental Grade initiation rituals. Although some of the material is familiar, there is much in the way of new data, instructions, and explanation of symbolism which has never been in print before now. Much of the information is from original Stella Matutina, Whare Ra, and Smaragdum Thalasses Inner Order Documents.

The GD rituals that have been published for the past fifty years are merely skeletons of the ceremonies. In other words, they explain merely what happens on the physical plane. These explanations came primarily from Z.1 and Z.5 documents, which were intended for the newly initiated Adeptus Minor who had just entered the Inner Order. The AM had just begun the Inner Order journey. It rather parallels the status of the Neophyte being newly initiated into the Outer Order.

The Inner Order documents presented in this and further volumes were intended for the seasoned Adept who was accomplished in the Inner Order procedures. The astral workings of the temple are described, as well as instructions on the god-form assumption and manipulation of the five currents of energy which are present in the 0=0 ceremony. For the first time, the currents of Aroueris, Isis, Nephthys, Thoth, and Osiris are described. As one reads this book and begins to understand the true meaning of the rituals, it becomes clear why the officers of the temple were to be trained Adepts. The balance, clarity, and power required to correctly perform the ceremonies are easily noticeable.

Also in the book, Zalewski describes in detail the manipulations of the Candidate's aura by the temple officers. How the individual currents affect the Candidate at each level of the ritual, how and when he is exposed to the Light of the Higher Self, and how he is protected at all times from the Evil Persona and any other negative forces is revealed. It gives one a sense of respect for the Adepts who perform the ritual and an understanding of the amount of time and effort spent to be able to perform it effectively.

Israel Regardie himself stated that a person could perform self initiation. He also mentioned personally to me that he felt that the Neophyte (0=0) initiation and the Adeptus Minor initiation rituals were of the utmost importance and should be experienced if the student had the opportunity to participate in them. With the information provided in this book, the reader may begin to see the true value these initiations play in the development of the student's psyche and subsequent evolution towards the Light and Conversation with the Holy Guardian Angel.

Regardie's own comments on the rituals are rather apt:

> From one point of view the officers employed in these Rituals represent just such psychic projections. They represent, even as figures in dreams do, different aspects of man himself— personifications of abstract psychological principles inhering within the human spirit. Through the admittedly artificial or conventional means of a dramatic projection of these personi-

fied principles in a well-ordered ceremony a reaction is induced in consciousness. This reaction is calculated to arouse from their dormant condition those hitherto latent faculties represented objectively in the Temple of Initiation by the officers. Without the least conscious effort on the part of the aspirant, an involuntary current of sympathy is produced by this external delineation of spiritual paths which may be sufficient to accomplish the purpose of the initiation ceremony. The aesthetic appeal to the imagination—quite apart from what could be called the intrinsic magical virtue with which the G.D. documents Z.1 and Z.3 deal at some length—stirs to renewed activity the life of the inner domain. And the entire action of this type of dramatic ritual is that the soul may discover itself exalted to the heights, and during that mystical elevation receive the rushing forth of the Light.[1]

The reader is about to view the 0=0 ceremony from a depth that was unavailable to either Regardie or Aleister Crowley. The magician will now be able to perform the ceremonies with much more understanding and effectiveness. With practice and perseverance, he/she has a great chance of fulfilling the purpose for which the rituals were originally designed.

I personally find the 0=0 ritual to be one of the most beautiful and moving ceremonies which a group can perform. In a full temple setting, with the Pillars, the robes, weapons, banners, and officers, it is something truly unique. When performed to its fullest potential, it affects not only the Candidate and the officers but all members present in the hall. When one is performing the role of an officer, the influx of energy and Light created brings one into direct contact with his/her spiritual potential and powers. Anyone wishing to achieve this state, and who is willing to persevere through a series of often dramatic transformations, will indeed be well rewarded by the greater awareness of his Higher Genius.

—Soror M.A.A.E.M., Co-Chief
Ra-Horakhty Temple
Hermetic Society of the Golden Dawn
Federal Way, Washington

---

[1]Regardie, Israel, *The Golden Dawn*, Llewellyn Publications, p. 27

Introduction

The concept of writing commentaries on the Neophyte Ritual (0=0) of the Golden Dawn was initially formulated as an Order document called the Z.5. We started writing this document in 1982, the year our Thoth-Hermes Temple was chartered by W. H. (Jack) Taylor. Taylor was a former Hierophant (of 7=4 grade) of the New Zealand Temple, Whare Ra. This temple was founded in 1912 by Dr. R. W. Felkin.

The Z.5 document was originally intended to be restricted to members of the Inner Order of Thoth-Hermes. It included many of the "word of mouth" teachings passed on by Taylor and other Inner Order Adepti from Whare Ra under whom we trained. The Z.5 was written to fill in information left out of two other Order papers, the Z.1 and Z.3. It also was designed to bridge the gap between the two papers.

The Z.1 paper is a technical explanation of the meanings and descriptions of the temple officers. The Z.3 is a clairvoyant description of the admission of the candidate. [The Z.1, Z.2, and Z.3 documents can be found in Book 5 of *The Golden Dawn*, edited by Israel Regardie, Llewellyn, 6th Edition, 1989. The Z.1 document is entitled "The Enterer of the Threshold." The Z.2 document is entitled "The Formulae of the Magic of Light," and the Z.3 is entitled "The Symbolism of the Admission of the Candidate."]

This book has been designed for the experienced Golden Dawn practitioner. It contains: 5=6 explanations of the 0=0 Ceremony, previously unpublished teachings from the 6=5 and 7=4 grades of the Stella Matutina, and later teachings from the Smaragdum Thalasses. "Smaragdum Thalasses" is the New Zealand name given to the order after Whare Ra withdrew from the Stella Matutina in 1933.

We have brought all of this information together in a unified format rather than stretch it out over the three Inner Order grades. Examples of this consolidation are given in "The Control and Functions of the Officers on the Dais," Chapter 2.

For some readers of this book, there may be areas that are initially incomprehensible. Dedicated reading and study will eventually bring an understanding of the material presented. For others, who have studied on their own or through various temples, we hope that the additional material will give more insight into the 0=0 grade.

When we first decided to do this book, we were faced with the problem of what to do with the existing Z.1 and Z.3 documents and their colorful but somewhat archaic language. We were not sure whether to rewrite them, omit them, use only our additional material, or leave them in and blend them in with the newer material so that the whole package could be presented in full. Ultimately, we chose the latter, which saved the reader from going book to book trying to fit the puzzle into place. In doing this, we have re-formatted the Z.1 and Z.3 documents to eliminate duplicate material. The importance of understanding the technical aspects of the Neophyte Ceremony cannot be overemphasized. It is the backbone of the Z.2 paper. This paper outlines ritual ceremony for Evocation, Consecration of Talismans, Invisibility, Transformations, Spiritual Development, Divination, and Alchemy. In the Neophyte Ritual of the Z.2, the Adept assumes the role of the Hierophant. The Hierophant must understand every aspect of what is happening in the ritual so that he/she can control the ceremony and give the forces life. He/she must also be able to dissect each layer of the ritual. If one area is lacking, he/she must be able to counterbalance the energies so that harmony prevails throughout the ceremony.

Both the Z.1 and the Z.3 documents were written very early in Golden Dawn history, around 1892 or earlier—barely four years after the first Neophyte Ceremony was conducted. After this, there was little input of this depth on the subject of the Neophyte ceremony by later Temples.

In 1903, the Golden Dawn split into two factions. The splinter group, led by Robert W. Felkin, formed the Stella Matutina, which retained the bulk of the Golden Dawn's Inner Order. Most members remained in the Order until World War I. Even in the 1920s, there were still some original Golden Dawn Adepti in the Stella Matutina. The 30 or so years of ritual experience gained in both Orders were shared with other Order members. A good example of this was the Hermes Temple in Bristol, England. During the 1930s, the Hermes Temple had a number of members who had been trained by Golden Dawn Adepti.

Israel Regardie, the editor of *The Golden Dawn* and several books on the Order, was a member of the Hermes Temple in Bristol during the 1930s. According to him, when questioned on this point in 1983, his only temple contacts during that time were with the Chiefs. He never met other members, though one person came to witness the consecration of his Elemental Weapons—which some, suprisingly enough, considered a major event in a temple. Because of this, Regardie was not aware that there were other members of the order with ritual experience.

Actually, the temple had a number of members with extensive ritual experience, but they had chosen to isolate themselves from other temple members during this time. Some of these members had been taught by Golden Dawn Adepti. Though well into their 70s, they were still actively engaged in Golden Dawn ritual.

The New Zealand Temple, Whare Ra, was also a good example of this cumulative type of teaching. Dr. Felkin was in charge of ritual training at Whare Ra. Under his guidance, Whare Ra members were the best trained in ritual magic of all the Golden Dawn temples, including the Hermes, Amoun, and Isis-Urania temples. This assertion is based on the opinions of visiting members of those temples who came to New Zealand.

Dr. Felkin ran ritual training in the New Zealand Order like a military operation. He went into extraordinary detail on how and what was happening. Around 1920, a former Golden Dawn Adept (from the old Isis-Urania Temple) and his wife visited Felkin in New Zealand. They expressed surprise at the ritual ability of some of the early Whare Ra Adepti. The training procedures advocated by Felkin, in their opinion, far outstripped those they had seen in the old Golden Dawn, as well as those of the American temples that they had previously visited.

In the late 1920s, a Whare Ra Adept by the name of Hugh (Euan) Campbell went to England to study the Dee manuscripts at the British Museum library for two years. While there, he became friendly with Langford Garstin, Chief of the Alpha et Omega (A.O.) Temple. Campbell's diary notes make the comment that the rituals in this temple were "slip shod" (he attended some Neophyte rituals and a 5=6 ritual) and lacked any real determined effort. Though Campbell was friendly with Garstin, he found that his Alpha et Omega Temple cousins treated rituals as a "chore that was simply tolerated." Garstin, in fact, tried to persuade the young New Zealander to stay in England and join his temple. Campbell had a high respect for Garstin, and found his ability and knowledge to be the exception rather than the rule in the A.O.

Whare Ra's isolation, in the small country village of Havelock North, had its advantages. A large number of this temple's founding group were extremely clairvoyant. When the temple was founded in 1912, Felkin found himself with a tight-knit group of religious devotees that had much to offer but no direction to go toward. When they applied themselves to the Golden Dawn rituals, it was done in the manner of religious fervor and fanaticism rarely seen outside the Middle Ages, and I make this comment with the greatest respect.

From 1912 until the 1940s, when Whare Ra was at its peak, much of this devotion to ritual produced some surprising results. For example, some Adepti would clairvoyantly check each other, during the performance of rituals, by viewing the state and color of the participants' auras.

My own experience of this type of checking procedure came from Jack Taylor. He used to make me create the temple god-forms of the 0=0 grade in the astral—with all the correct coloring. He would then proceed to check each one and give a comment on whether it was correct or not. If not, I would then have to start again. One day, I decided to test him on this by creating the form of a lion in the Invisible Station of Horus. When he got to this form he told me, rather dryly, that I should try a little further north—like Egypt —and leave the rest of the pride behind. I never again tested his abilities. Admittedly, abilities such as Taylor demonstrated were rare, but the number who possessed this in the early days of Whare Ra was quite abnormally high when compared to other temples.

I do not wish to give the impression that the greater number of Whare Ra Adepts knew more about ritual than their old Golden Dawn counterparts, because they did not. However, an inner core did exist who excelled in ritual work.

Whare Ra members were taught courses in Tarot, astrology, and Enochian work, along with the Z.2 documents, which were optional studies. The first things taught new members, however, were the mechanics of ritual. Some older members considered these to be of singular importance, and taught them to the detriment of the other studies. Students were required to keep their eyes on the cracks of the concrete to locate exact places to stand and walk during the rituals. This caused a great deal of pressure on Adepti and a number left the Order because of it. Those who survived under this type of training were mostly strict disciplinarians.

Before World War II, training by word of mouth was quite detailed, and it produced a number of Adepts of high caliber. In the final stage of Whare Ra's existence, however, from 1959 to the temple's end in the late 1970s, this method of training deteriorated, and the temple failed to produce the skilled leadership needed to sustain it. Ritual training was inadequate and lacked the necessary supplemental support of the Z papers. Adepti had to write their own papers and formulate their own opinions as to what went on. As a result, the last three Chiefs of the Order were unable to reach the skill level of previous Chiefs, and the temple disbanded.

It is unfortunate that, in the final days of the temple, members with the most ritual understanding failed to rise to any real position of power. Those who were in charge had little knowledge to pass on to others—with the exceptions of Taylor, Campbell, and one or two others. This was aptly illustrated by a humorous anecdote related to us by a couple that belonged to the temple during its final stages.

The couple reported that they had been instructed by a former late Chief to "walk like an Egyptian" during rituals. The couple, puzzled by what this meant, asked for further illumination. The Chief, obviously unsure of what it meant herself, ignored their request. When we heard this, we were reminded of the pop tune and video of the same name by the Bangles. To this day, we cannot hear the tune nor watch the video without bursting into laughter.

When we first got interested in magic, we studied the Golden Dawn rituals from Regardie's published works. When put to the practical test, this information on rituals left quite a number of questions unanswered. It was not until our period with Taylor, and also other Adepti who helped, that we began to truly understand ritual work and record this understanding on paper. We began to feel like Carlos Castaneda felt in the presence of Don Juan (see *The Teachings of Don Juan: A Yaqui Way of Knowledge*) and were forever taking notes on instructions, conversation and general folklore from Whare Ra. We knew that the opportunity we had was a once-in-a-lifetime experience and should not be lost. We found that we virtually had to start again from scratch.

As we conducted the physical actions of each ceremony, we had to learn the functions on the many different levels of the astral, about which virtually nothing had been written in the published papers of the Order. This type of teaching was the "word of mouth" type that had been handed down from Hierophant to Hierophant since the formation of the Order in England.

Over the years of our association with Taylor one thing became obvious—we had much to learn about ritual work. We were extremely fortunate to come under Taylor's wing. We also were enriched by our acquaintance with the elite circle of ex-Inner Order Whare Ra members, who continually helped us and gave us advice over the years.

It is unfortunate that some of the published comments about the

Stella Matutina are blatantly contemptuous. Reading these ac-
counts, one would consider that most of the members were a bunch
of incompetents who were mixing in things they knew little about.
Most of this stemmed from Regardie's comments of his experiences
in the Hermes Temple and the tampering with the ritual documents. This, however, was not always the case in the New Zealand
Temple. While it is true that their scholarship left a lot to be desired
in some areas of the Order's teaching, they were quite exceptional at
ritual magic.

The best I have ever seen was Taylor, and the members of the
Order of the Table Round. This was a small Arthurian Order that
Felkin brought to New Zealand along with the Golden Dawn. It had
a large number of Whare Ra, Inner Order, members within it.

When we were initiated into this side Order (before we were
initiated into the Golden Dawn, or the Smaragdum Thalasses, as it is
called in New Zealand), all those on the dais and most of the floor
officers were Inner Order Golden Dawn members as well. This was
a totally different experience from any dry Masonic type Order that
we had experienced before. Here, it seemed to us, was ritual magic
in its essence. The experiences at the hands of this well-drilled
collection of officers left their mark on us. While we had practiced
Golden Dawn rituals before, they were nothing compared to this
level. The problem, of course, was our own lack of experience and
our inability to recognize the ritualistic signposts.

Over the next few years we found we were swamped with the
amount of unpublished material on these rituals. Taylor, to my
mind, was something of a ritualistic genius who could dissect and
instantly point to the problem. One of his favorite anecdotes was a
conversation he had with Mrs. Felkin back in the 1930s. Jack
commented, after a Neophyte practice, that everyone had managed
their parts without making a mistake. Mrs. Felkin countered that
there might have been perfection in the rendition, but there had
been no power to the ritual. Jack had to agree. It was this type of
mechanical approach to ritual on the mundane level that Taylor
abhorred. He tried to make all those he taught look deeper into
themselves.

Although learning about ritual magic from books such as this leaves a lot to be desired, it is often the only way to learn the subject, especially when a teacher is not available. This book is a tool, and a helpful guide based on the observations of a number of Adepts from the Golden Dawn, the Stella Matutina, and the Smaragdum Thalasses. It has been designed to make you aware of certain areas of importance in ritual. But only your own training and practice will make some of the things described here happen.

We have chosen the Neophyte Ceremony for the first of our books on ritual, because it is the essence of the Z.2 rituals from which all of the Second Order Rituals are based. To understand and perform the Z.2 correctly, one must know the higher functions of the Neophyte Ceremony.

Within the Golden Dawn teachings, within the "word of mouth" category, is the continual reference to magnetic manipulation of the aura. This starts at the Neophyte grade and continues through the 7=4 grade. Some of the "word of mouth" techniques, taught to us by Taylor, go back to the old Golden Dawn. However, we have taken the liberty of expanding them somewhat in this book. Eliphas Levi says in his *Transcendental Magic.*

> When the magus has attained lucidity, whether through the mediation of a pythoness or by his own development, he communicates and directs at will the magnetic vibrations in the whole mass of the Astral Light, the currents of which he divines by means of the Magic Wand, which is a perfected divining rod. By the aid of these vibrations he influences the nervous system of persons made subject to his action, accelerates or suspends the currents of life, soothes or tortures, heals or hurts—in fine, slays or brings to life. . . .

This is possibly an oversimplification. However, it is a highly accurate statement of the actions of ritual magic and the actions of the Hierophant and his Scepter during a ceremony such as that of the Neophyte. Just by studying the magnetic actions alone, one enters a labyrinth world of magnetism that has many layers. Some of these we hope to discuss in this book.

Over twenty years ago, I studied Tantra under the late Vivan-datta. He made me aware of the use of the auric energies of the body.

He used his own aura to magnetically increase his body's vibrational pitch and thus sensitize it to certain etheric fields. This is where teachers like Taylor, who have the same ability as Vivandatta to control their aura, could teach at their best. They would not only tell you, they would show you. Taylor had the ability to take you out of your own physical body and introduce you to the magnetic currents in the ritual, one level at a time. The experience has to be undergone to be believed. But in doing this, he demonstrated a power that I have never perceived in any other magician before. He was truly awesome in this field, something which went against his frail body which was confined to a wheelchair in his twilight years.

When doing ritual, there is no substitute for practice. At Whare Ra, whenever possible, ritual practice was done once a week. Some temples train just once a month with only the officers conducting the ceremony attending. We would suggest that once a week be the average, with as many people as will fit into the Hall. Have those present take notes on their impressions of the movements, errors, and so on. This keeps everyone alert during the proceedings. The mechanics can be quickly learned this way. Furthermore, it leaves the way free for everyone to concentrate on the inner mechanisms. It is no good saying after the ritual that "it was really powerful this time." Rather, everyone must be able to dissect it and say why it was powerful or why the power was lacking. Ritual training is very hard work, make no mistake about it. People get quickly bored if they are half-hearted about it.

In this book there are a number of old concepts that have never been publicly revealed before and many new ones that we have developed. We hope that, over the years, others will benefit from our experiences and eventually improve on our meager notes. We are fast approaching an age where instruments, whether electronic, radionic, or a combination of both, will be able to categorize precisely the various energy levels during different parts of the ritual. The future adept may be able to use these, like biofeedback principles, to improve his or her performance. Until then, there is still a lot of hard work ahead of us. For those of you who may wish to study the magnetic theory from the scientific viewpoint of radionics, we would suggest reading David V. Tansley's book, *Radionics*

Interface with the Ether Fields, especially the chapter on the "Geometric Etheric Link."

This book has been divided into two parts. Part one gives the 0=0 ritual, which is taken from one of Whare Ra's earliest documents. It was written around 1912. When Whare Ra withdrew from the Stella Matutina in 1933, the rituals then simply crossed out the words "Stella Matutina" and inserted "Smaragdum Thalasses." This copy belonged to a former Chief of that Temple, Mason Chambers. He was one of the three Chiefs that Felkin left in charge, when he returned to England after his initial visit to New Zealand. When compared to previously published versions of the ritual, by Regardie, Torrens, and Gilbert, one will find, in some instances, additional material on the pivots, turns, etc., but also there are some areas lacking. There is an Alternate Adoration, given here, which was left up to the discretion of the Hierophant to use. In addition, more information is provided on the ceremony of the Eucharist, at the end of the ceremony, which has not been published before.

Overall, it would be a fair comment to say that the Stella Matutina versions of the Neophyte Rituals are far more descriptive than the early Golden Dawn ones that have been examined. A comparison with the published versions of both Torrens and Regardie will bear this out. The reason for this is unclear. It is possible they were re-edited by a group of Adepti under the Morgan Rothe (M.R.), the name for the Order between 1900 and 1903. "Morgan Rothe" is a Germanic name which loosely translates as "Red Dawn."

There are a number of other possibilities for the discrepancies in the versions. Perhaps the papers were re-edited later by the Stella Matutina, or the temple copies from the original master copies of Mathers were condensed to save additional writing.

Another version of the Neophyte Ceremony, written three years after the original breakup of the Order in 1900, is published by R.A. Gilbert in his *Golden Dawn: Twilight of the Magicians.* This is, in some respects, closer to, though not identical with, the New Zealand version published here.

Part two gives the explanation in a step-by-step easy-to-follow format. The whole book is designed to show the type of procedure a person encounters when joining a Golden Dawn Temple.

On a final note, there are a number of purists who go against any tampering with the Golden Dawn rituals. In the past, some of this tampering has been inferior and deserved criticism. In other areas, such as the Consecration Rituals of the Elemental Weapons, the changes made by the Stella Matutina, in the Hermes Temple at Bristol, were superior to the original Golden Dawn documents. This is a point that most Golden Dawn aspirants will agree on, though each case must be presented on its own merits.

Some years ago, I had a discussion with a high-ranking member of the Order who took great pains to point out the "absolute correctness of the Consecration of the Vault Ceremony" after I suggested a change to it without telling this person what the change was. After some deliberation, this person was rather red-faced when informed that the consecration of Fire and Water was done in the reverse manner to what it should be, a basic error of some importance in a very important ceremony. Perfection in ritual is a goal to be strived for, and to do this one must be constantly trying to improve on the old to make it better where possible. But change in this area must be made for all the right reasons, and not for change's sake alone. The Golden Dawn is no exception. Some may consider that we have complicated an already complex system. For example, in our own case, when we were first introduced to many of the "word of mouth" teachings, we had our fair share of headaches trying to fathom out the intricacy of Golden Dawn ritual work. On more than one occasion, we wondered whether this was all necessary. Taylor put this to us very simply:

> If you do not understand the deeper meaning of ritual, whether it be Golden Dawn or otherwise, then all you are doing is marking time and not growing in this area. The human soul and its connection to ritual is more complex that we have even dreamed about and, if you want to get to the kernel of this, then you will have to work long and hard. Even though I am now 87, and have been doing Golden Dawn ritual work for nearly 60 years, I still learn more every time I read or study the rituals. My own teacher told me years ago to make the complex second nature and then will you start to understand the deeper meaning of ritual.

We in New Zealand have not tried to set ourselves up as the last word on Golden Dawn ritual teachings. But we have tried, in our own way, to present some of the information we have learned to Golden Dawn enthusiasts. This needed to be done, for Whare Ra lasted the longest of the Golden Dawn temples. If we had waited for some elderly members of the Hermes-Bristol Temple to break their quarter of a century of silence and publish a volume such as this, I feel we should have a long wait.

If there are Golden Dawn Temples like our Thoth-Hermes that are there by "Apostolic Succession" and have the training and knowledge to pass on information and are reticent through their Obligation, then I make no apology for this work because they have preferred to keep the information to themselves at the expense of others who wish to learn. Personally, I find this type of attitude intolerable, especially in this day and age. To my mind, this is taking a step back to the dark ages of occultism. This information, which is slowly but surely making its way to the general public, is becoming an almost unstoppable tide. It is quite obvious to many that this is the way in which the Golden Dawn can be brought into the 21st century.

—Pat Zalewski
Wellington, New Zealand

Part 1
The Ritual

The Neophyte Ritual of Whare Ra Temple

0=0 Grade of the First Order of the Stella Matutina

Officers

Imperator, Praemonstrator, Cancellarius
Hierophant—red robe, lamen, crown-headed scepter.
Hiereus   —black robe, lamen, sword.
Hegemon   —white robe, lamen, mitre-headed scepter.
Kerux   —lamen, lamp, wand.
Stolistes   —lamen, cup of lustral water.
Dadouchos —lamen, thurbile.
Sentinel   —lamen, sword.

Requirements

Red rose, cross, triangle, chalice, paten, salt, bread, lamp, hoodwink, sample sash, chemical change, and roll of membership.

Opening

When members are assembled and clothed, Hierophant gives one knock. Kerux (Kerukains) goes to right of Hierophant, faces West, elevates wand and says:—

Kerux: *Hekas, Hekas, Este Bebeloi.*

Kerux returns to his place by East and South, giving the Grade Sign as he passes the Throne of the East. (N.B.: In all movements of officers and members the course of the Sun—a clockwise direction—must be followed, except in reverse circumambulation, though it may not invariably be necessary to pass immediately in front of the Hierophant; but, when this latter is done, the Grade Salute must be given, as also when well within the Portal on entering or leaving the Hall. The Grade sign must be made in the direction of movement—clockwise, except when entering or leaving the Hall, when it is made towards the Hierophant.)

Hierophant rises with one knock.

Hiero: *Fratres and Sorores of the Order of the Stella Matutina, assist me to open the Hall of the Neophytes.*

All rise.

> *Frater Kerux, see that the Hall is properly guarded.*

Kerux ascertains that the Hall is properly guarded by giving one knock—or he unlocks the door, looks out, then recloses and relocks the door. Sentinel replies by giving one knock with the hilt of his sword. (This applies also to closing.) If Sentinel is not present, Kerux gives one knock in reply to himself.

Kerux: *Very Honored Hierophant, the Hall is properly guarded.*

Hiero: *Honored Hiereus, guard the hither side of the Portal and assure yourself that all present have beheld the Morning Star.*

Hiereus passes to the door, stands in front of it with sword, Kerux at his right hand with lamp and wand.

Hiereus: *Fratres and Sorores of the Order of the Stella Matutina, give the Signs of the Neophyte.*

Done. Hiereus gives Signs.

Very Honored Hierophant, all present have been so honored.

Hiereus returns to his place. The Hierophant repeats the Signs.

Hiero: *Let the number of Officers of the Grade and the nature of their offices be proclaimed once again, that the powers whose images they are may be re-awakened in the spheres of those now present and in the sphere of this Order, for by names and images are all powers awakened and re-awakened.*

Gives Sign of Silence.

Honored Hiereus, how many Chief Officers are there in this Grade?

Hiereus: *There are three Chief Officers: the Hierophant, Hiereus, and Hegemon.* (Hierophantria, Hiereia, and Hegemone, if they are feminine.)

Hiero: *Is there any peculiarity in these Names?*

Hiereus: *They all commence with the letter 'H.'*

Hiero: *And of what is this Letter a symbol?*

Hiereus: *Of Life, because the letter 'H' is our mode of representing the ancient Greek aspirate or breathing, and Breath is evidence of Life.*

Hiero: *How many lesser Officers are there?*

Hiereus: *There are three besides the Sentinel: Kerux (Kerukaina), Stolistes (Stolistria), and Dadouchos (Dadouche). The Sentinel guards the Portal of the Hall and has a sword in his hand to keep out intruders. It is his duty to prepare the Candidate.*

Hiero: *Frater Dadouchos, your station and duties?*

Dadouchos: *My station is in the South to symbolize Heat and Dryness, and my duty is to see that the Lamp and Fires of the Temple are ready at the Opening, and to watch over the Censer and Incense, and to consecrate the Hall and the*

Fratres and Sorores and the Candidate with Fire.

Hiero: *Frater Stolistes, your station and duties?*

Stolistes: *My station is in the North, to symbolize Cold and Moisture, and my duties are to see that the Robes and Collars and Insignia of the Officers are ready at the Opening, and to watch over the Cup of Lustral Water and to purify the Hall and the Fratres and Sorores and the Candidate with Water.*

Hiero: *Frater Kerux, your station and duties?*

Kerux: *My station is within the Portal; my duties are to see that the furniture of the Hall is properly arranged at the Opening, and to guard the inner side of the Portal, to admit Fratres and Sorores, and to watch over the reception of the Candidate, and to lead all mystic Circumambulations, carry the Lamp of my Office, and to make all reports and announcements. My Lamp is a symbol of the Hidden Knowledge and my Wand is a symbol of its directing power.*

Hiero: *Honored Hegemon, your station and duties?*

Hegemon: *My station is between the Two Pillars of Hermes and Solomon, and my face is towards the Cubical Altar of the Universe. My duty is to watch over the Gateway of the Hidden Knowledge, for I am the Reconciler between Light and Darkness. I watch over the reception of the Candidate and his preparation, and I lead him in the Path that conducts from Darkness to Light. The White Color of my robe is the color of Purity, my ensign of office is a Mitre-headed scepter to symbolize religion which guides and regulates life, and my Office symbolizes those higher Aspirations of the Soul which should guide its actions.*

Hiero: *Honored Hiereus, your station and duties?*

Hiereus: *My station is on the Throne of the West and is a symbol of increase of Darkness and decrease of Light, and I am the Master of Darkness. I keep the Gateway of the West and watch over the reception of the Candidate and over lesser*

Officers in the doing of their work. My black Robe is an image of the darkness that was upon the face of the Waters. I carry the sword of Judgment and the banner of the Evening Twilight, which is the Banner of the West, and I am called Fortitude by the Unhappy.

Hiero: *My station is on the Throne of the East in the place where the Sun rises, and I am Master of the Hall, governing it according to the Laws of the Order, as HE whose image I am, is the Master of all who work for the Hidden Knowledge. My robe is red because of Uncreated Fire and Created Fire, and I hold the Scepter of Power and the Banner of the Morning Light, which is the Banner of the East. I am called Power and Mercy and Light and Abundance, and I am the Expounder of the Mysteries.*

   Frater Stolistes, I command you to purify the Hall and members with Water.

Stolistes goes to the East and faces Hierophant, salutes, and makes a cross with Cup and sprinkles thrice with first and second fingers and thumb of right hand. Passes to South, West, and North, facing each point as he repeats cross and sprinkling, completes circle by returning to East where he faces East and says:—

   I purify with Water.

Salutes Throne and returns to place by South and West.

Hiero: *Frater Dadouchos, I command you to consecrate the Hall and members with Fire.*

Dadouchos passes by West and North to East, faces Hierophant, salutes, holds thurible chain short and makes a cross, then lengthens the chain and censes with three forward swings, passes South, West, and North, facing each point, making a cross and three swings, completes circle by returning East, faces Hierophant and raises the thurible on high saying:—

   I consecrate with Fire.

Salutes Throne and returns to place direct.
Kerux goes to North, near Stolistes, facing East.

Hiero: *Let the Mystic Circumambulation take place in the Pathway of LIGHT.*

In the following order: Hegemon, Hiereus, Members, Stolistes, Dadouchos, Kerux, and Sentinel last. In forming procession, Kerux passes to North, halts; Hegemon passes by South and West where he is joined by Hiereus, carrying the Banner of the West in his left hand and sword in his right; they pass on, Hegemon in front of Hiereus, and take their places behind Kerux; Dadouchos follows Hegemon from South, joining Stolistes; members from up behind Hiereus, Stolistes being on the left of Dadouchos (If too many members, officers only go around). As each passes Banner of East, he salutes in the Direction of progress. Hiereus passes Hierophant once, Hegemon twice, and the rest three times, and then all return to places. Hierophant stands with Banner of the East in his left hand and his scepter in his right.

Hiero: *The Mystical Circumambulation symbolical of the rise of LIGHT is accomplished. Let us adore the Lord of the Universe and Spaces.*

All turn East and salute, repeating the salute at each adoration, then give the Sign of Silence. Remain bent over until final Sign.

Hiero: *Holy are Thou, Lord of the Universe!* (Salute)
Holy are Thou, Whom Nature hath not formed! (Salute)
Holy are Thou, the Vast and the Mighty One! (Salute)
Lord of the Light and of the Darkness!
(Salute with Sign of Silence)

All officers raise Banners, Scepters, etc., on high then sink them in salutation.

Hiero: *Frater Kerux, in the name of the Lord of the Universe, who works in Silence, whom naught but Silence can express, I command you to declare that I have opened the Hall of the*

Neophytes.

Kerux passes Northeast in front of Hierophant's Throne, faces West, and raises his wand.

Kerux: *In the name of the Lord of the Universe, Who works in Silence and Whom naught but Silence can express, I declare that the Day Star has arisen and the Shadows flee away.*

Hiero: (knocks)

Hiereus: (knocks)

Hegemon: (knocks)

Hiero: (knocks) *KHABS.*

Hiereus: (knocks) *AM.*

Hegemon: (knocks) *PEKHT.*

Hiereus: (knocks) *KONX.*

Hegemon: (knocks) *OM.*

Hiero: (knocks) *PAX.*

Hegemon: (knocks) *LIGHT.*

Hiero: (knocks) *IN.*

Hiereus: (knocks) *EXTENSION.*

All make Signs and resume seats.
Kerux removes Rose, Lamp, Chalice, and paten from Altar.
Minutes of the last meeting read and confirmed, Work of the Grade gone through, resolutions passed, etc.

Ceremony of Admission

The Candidate is not to be told the name of the Order of the Stella Matutina until his admission.

Hiero: *Fratres et Sorores of the Order of the Stella Matutina, I have received a Dispensation from the greatly Honored Chiefs of the Second Order, to admit _____ to the 0=0*

Grade of Neophyte. Honored Hegemon, bid the Candidate prepare for the Ceremony of his admission, and superintend his preparation.

Hegemon rises, removes chair from between the Pillars, and going without the Portal sees that Sentinel hoodwinks candidate and binds a rope three times round his waist. Hegemon takes the candidate by his right hand with his own left and causes him to knock.

Kerux: *The Candidate seeks for entrance.* (turns down lights)

Hiero: *I give permission to admit* _____, *who now loses his name and will be henceforth known among us as* _____. *Let the Stolistes and the Dadouchos assist the Kerux in his reception.*

Candidate is now inside the Portal.

Hegemon: *Inheritor of a Dying World (or, Child of Earth; or, ye Earth-born folk), arise and enter the Darkness.*

Stolistes: *The Mother of Darkness hath blinded him with her Hair.*

Dadouchos: *The Father of darkness hath hidden him under His wings.*

Hiero: *His limbs are still weary from the wars which were in Heaven.*

Kerux: *Unconsecrated and Unpurified, thou cans't not enter our Sacred Hall.*

Stolistes marks forehead with a cross and sprinkles thrice.

Stolistes: *I purify thee with Water.*

Dadouchos makes a cross and censes thrice.

Dadouchos: *I consecrate thee with Fire.*

Should there be more than one Candidate, Stolistes and Dadouchos must consecrate each alternately, so as to complete one before going to the next. Stolistes and Dadouchos resume places, going clockwise but remaining standing.

Hiero: *Conduct the Candidate to the foot of the Altar.*
Inheritor of a Dying World, why seekest thou to enter our
Sacred Hall? Why seekest thou admission to our Order?

Hegemon: (for Candidate) *My Soul wanders in Darkness and*
seeks the Light of the Hidden Knowledge, and I believe that
in this Order, the Knowledge of that ancient Light may be
obtained.

Hiero: *We hold your written pledge to keep secret everything that*
relates to this Order. To confirm it, I now ask you, are you
willing to take the solemn Obligation in the presence of this
Assembly, to keep the secrets and Mysteries of our Order
inviolate? There is nothing incompatible with your civil,
moral, or religious duties in this Obligation. Although the
Magical virtues can indeed awaken into momentary Life in
the wicked and foolish hearts, they cannot reign in any heart
that has not the natural virtues to be their throne. He who is
the Fountain of the Spirit of Man and of Things, came not to
break, but to fulfill the Law. Are you ready to take this Oath?

Candidate: *I am ready.*

Hiereus, Hierophant, and Hegemon take their places in the form
of a triangle around the Altar, Hierophant, from the East,
advancing between the Pillars with scepter. Hiereus, North-
West of Altar with sword. Hegemon, Southwest of Altar with
scepter. Dadouchos East of Hegemon, and Stolistes East of
Hiereus. Candidate, West of Altar. All members stand.

Hiero: *Kneel on both your knees.*

Candidate is assisted.

Give me your right hand which I place upon this Holy
Symbol. Place your left hand in mine, bow your head, repeat
your full name by which you are known on earth, and say
after me:
    I _____ in the Presence of the LORD of the Universe, Who

works in Silence and whom naught but Silence can express, and in this Hall of the Neophytes of the STELLA MATUTINA, regularly assembled under warrant from the Greatly Honored Chiefs of the Second Order, do of my own free will, hereby and hereon, most solemnly promise to keep secret this Order, its Name, the Names of its Members and the proceedings that take place at its meetings, from every person in the world who has not been initiated into it: nor will I discuss them with any member who has not the Password for the time being, or who has resigned, demitted, or been expelled.

I undertake to maintain a kindly and benevolent relation with all the Fratres and Sorores of this Order.

I solemnly promise to keep secret any information I may have gathered concerning this Order before taking this Oath.

I solemnly promise that any Ritual or lecture placed in my care or any cover containing them, shall bear the official label of this Order.

I will neither copy nor allow to be copied any manuscript, until I have obtained permission of the Second Order, lest our Secret Knowledge be revealed through my neglect.

I solemnly promise not to suffer myself to be placed in such a state of passivity, that any uninitiated person may cause me to lose control of my words or actions.

I solemnly promise to persevere with courage and determination in the labors of the Divine Science, even as I shall persevere with courage and determination through this Ceremony which is their Image—and I will not debase my mystical knowledge in the labor of Evil Magic at any time tried or under any temptation.

I swear upon this Holy Symbol to observe all these things without evasion, equivocation, or mental reservation, under the penalty of being expelled from this Order for my perjury and my offence, and furthermore submitting myself by my own consent to a Deadly Stream of Power, set in action by the Divine Guardians of this Order, Who, Living the Light of their Perfect Justice, can, as tradition and experience affirm, strike the breaker of this Magical Obligation with death or palsy, or overwhelm him with misfortune. They journey as upon the Winds; they strike where no man strikes; they slay where no man slays.

Hiereus places sword on Candidate's neck.

As I bow my neck under the Sword of the Hiereus, so do I commit myself unto their hands for vengeance or reward. So help me my Mighty and Secret Soul, and the Father of my Soul Who works in Silence and Whom naught but Silence can express.

Hiero: *Rise now Neophyte of the 0=0 Grade of the Order of the Stella Matutina.*

Hierophant resumes Throne.

Honored Hegemon will you now place the Neophyte in the Northern part of the Hall—the place of Forgetfulness, Dumbness, and Necessity, and of the greatest symbolical Darkness.

Hegemon does so, facing Candidate to East.

Hiero: *The Voice of my Undying Soul and Secret Soul said unto me, "Let me enter the Path of Darkness and peradventure, there shall I find the Light. I am the only Being in the Abyss of Darkness; from an Abyss of Darkness came I forth ere my birth, from the Silence of a Primal Sleep. And the Voice of Ages said unto my Soul—"I am He who formulates in Darkness, the Light that shineth in Darkness, yet the Darkness comprehendeth it not."*

Let the Mystic Circumambulation take place in the Path of Darkness which leads unto the Light, with the Lamp of the Hidden Knowledge to guide us.

Dadouchos moves round by West to North and as soon as he has ranged himself on the right hand of the Stolistes, Kerux takes his place in front of Hegemon and Neophyte, and Kerux, Hegemon with Neophyte, Stolistes and Dadouchos pass round the Hall. At their first passing, Hiereus gives one knock. At their second passing Hierophant gives one knock. After the second passing of Hierophant, as soon as they reach the South, Kerux turns and bars the way.

Kerux: *Unpurified and Unconsecrated, thou cannot enter the Path of the West!*

Stolistes and Dadouchos come forward and Stolistes marks a cross on the forehead and sprinkles thrice.

Stolistes: *I purify thee with Water.*

Dadouchos waves censer in the form of a cross and swings it thrice.

Dadouchos: *I consecrate thee with Fire.*

Stolistes and Dadouchos fall back to their places in the rear.

Hegemon: *Child of Earth (or Mortal born of Earth) twice purified and twice consecrated thou mayest approach the pathway of the West.*

Kerux leads procession to Throne of Hiereus, who threatens with Sword.

Hiereus: *Thou canst not pass by me, saith the Guardian of the West, unless thou can tell me my name.*

Hegemon: *Darkness is thy Name, thou Great One of the Paths of the Shades.*

Kerux lifts hoodwink for a moment.

Hiereus: *Fear is failure, so be thou without fear. For he that trembles at the Flame and at the Flood and at the Shadows of the Air, hath no part in GOD. Thou hast known me now, so pass thou on.*

Kerux replaces hoodwink, procession moves on past Hierophant, who gives one knock, and past Hiereus, who knocks again. Arriving at North, Kerux turns and bars the way.

Kerux: *Unpurified and Unconsecrated, thou canst not enter the Pathway of the East.*

Stolistes and Dadouchos consecrate as before.

Hegemon: *Thrice purified and thrice consecrated, thou mayest approach the Gateway of the East.*

Stolistes and Dadouchos retire to rear. Kerux leads procession to Hierophant, who rises and menaces with scepter.

Hiero: *Thou canst not pass me, saith the Guardian of the East, unless thou canst tell me my name.*

Hegemon: *Light dawning in Darkness is thy Name, the Light of a Golden Day.*

Kerux raises hoodwink for a moment.

Hiero: *Unbalanced Power is the ebbing away of Life. Unbalanced Mercy is weakness and the fading out of the Will. Unbalanced Severity is cruelty and the barrenness of the mind. Thou hast known me now, so pass thou on to the cubical Altar of the Universe.*

Kerux replaces hoodwink and leads procession to Altar. Hierophant leaves Throne and passes between Pillars with scepter in his right hand and Banner of East in his left. He stops either between the Pillars or halfway between them and the Altar, or else to the east of the Altar, saying, halting at each sentence:—

Hiero: *I come in the Power of the Light;*
I come in the Light of Wisdom;
I come in the Mercy of the Light;
The Light has Healing in his Wings.

Hiereus takes his place North of the Altar; Hegemon South and Neophyte West. Kerux behind Neophyte, between him and the Throne of the West. Stolistes West of Hiereus and Dadouchos West of Hegemon. All officers and members kneel. Hierophant turns to Altar, standing, and says:—

Hiero: *Lord of the Universe—the Vast and Mighty One;*
Ruler of the Light and of the Darkness;
We adore Thee and we invoke Thee;
Look with favor upon this Neophyte who kneeleth before Thee, and grant Thine aid unto the higher aspirations of his (her) Soul, so that he (she) may prove a true and faithful Frater (Soror) Neophyte among us; to the glory of Thine Ineffable Name. Amen!

Alternate Invocation
Oh Thou Whom nature hath not Formed;
Oh Thou Who didst in reason Constitute the things that are;
Oh Thou Whom nought but Silence can Express;
Look with favor upon this Neophyte; grant that he may labor in high things. Accept the pure offering of his reason from heart and soul stretched up to Thee. Let him become a faithful Frater (Soror) among us to Thy glory and to the glory of Thy Hierarchies. Amen!

All rise and remain standing. Neophyte is assisted to rise. Hierophant comes close to Altar and raises his scepter above Neophyte's head. Hiereus raises sword so as to touch Hierophant's scepter. Hegemon raises his scepter to others. Kerux then removes hoodwink at the word "light."

Hiero: *Inheritor of a Dying World, we call thee to the Living Beauty.*

Hiereus: *Wanderer in Wild Darkness, we call thee to the Gentle Light."*

Sentinel turns up Lights.

Hiero: *Long has thou dwelt in Darkness—Quit the Night and seek the Day.*

All: *We receive thee into the Order of the Stella Matutina.*

Hiero: (knocks) *KHABS.*

Hiereus: (knocks) *AM.*

Hegemon: (knocks) *PEKHT.*

Hiereus: (knocks) *KONX.*

Hegemon: (knocks) *OM.*

Hiero: (knocks) *PAX.*

Hegemon: (knocks) *LIGHT.*

Hiero: (knocks) *IN.*

Hiereus: (knocks) *EXTENSION.*

Officers remove scepters and sword from head of Neophyte. Kerux goes Northeast, raising lamp on high.

Hiero: (points to Kerux) *In all thy wandering in Darkness, the Lamp of the Kerux went before thee, though it was not seen by thine eyes. It is a symbol of the Light of the Hidden Knowledge. Let the Neophyte be led to the East of the Altar.*

Hegemon leads Neophyte to the North and East, placing him between the Pillars.

Hiero: *Honored Hiereus, give the Secret Sign, Token and Words, together with the present Password of the 0=0 Grade of the Stella Matutina. Place him (her) between the Mystic Pillars and superintend his (her) fourth and final Consecration.*

Hiereus passes by North to Black Pillar and stands on East side of it, facing Neophyte. Hegemon takes up similar position by White Pillar. Hiereus gives sword and banner to Hegemon and then stands in front of and facing Neophyte, passing between Pillars to do so.

Hiereus: *Frater (Soror) _____, I shall now proceed to instruct you in the secret Signs, grip and Words of this Grade. Firstly, advance thy left foot a pace as if entering a portal. This is the Step.*
    The Signs are two. The First or Saluting Sign is given thus: lean forward and stretch out both arms thus: It alludes to your condition in a state of darkness groping for Light. The

second Sign is the Sign of Silence, and is given by placing the left forefinger on your lip thus: Left forefinger upon lower lip. It is the position shown in many ancient statues of Harpocrates and it alludes to the strict silence you have sworn to maintain concerning everything connected with this Order. The first sign is always answered by the second.

The Grip or Token is given thus: advance your left foot touching mine, toe and heel, extend your right hand to grasp mine, fail, try again, and then succeed in touching the fingers only. It alludes to the seeking guidance in Darkness.

The Grand Word is Har-Par-Krat, and is whispered in this position mouth to ear, in syllables. It is the Egyptian name for the God of Silence, and should always remind you of the strict silence you have sworn to maintain.

The Password is ____. It is periodically changed each Equinox so that a Member who has resigned, demitted, or been expelled may be ignorant of the existing Password. I now place you between the two Pillars of Hermes and Solomon in the symbolic gateway of Occult Wisdom.

Hiereus takes Neophyte by hands and draws him forward until he is between the Pillars. He takes back sword and banner from Hegemon, returns to his position North of and close to the Black Pillar, and says:—

Hiereus: *Let the final Consecration take place.*

Kerux goes to the North and remains there until the procession is formed. Stolistes and Dadouchos purify and consecrate the Hall as in the Opening, but at the end, instead of facing the Hierophant and raising the cup and censer on high, each salutes the Hierophant and then turns and consecrates Neophyte as previously.

Stolistes: *I purify thee with Water.*

Dadouchos: *I consecrate thee with Fire.*

Hiero: *Honored Hegemon, I command you to remove the Rope, last remaining symbol of the Path of Darkness, and to invest our*

Frater (Soror) with the badge of this degree.

Hegemon passes from behind the White Pillar, hands scepter to Hiereus, removes rope, and invests Neophyte.

Hegemon: *By command of the Very Honored Hierophant, I invest you with the Badge of this degree. It symbolizes Light dawning in Darkness.*

Hegemon returns to White Pillar.

Hiero: *Let the Mystic Circumambulation take place in the Pathway of Light.*

Hierophant stands as in Opening, Hegemon in front and leading Neophyte, behind Kerux, Hiereus and then members and finally Dadouchos and Stolistes. All salute when passing Hierophant. Hiereus drops out when procession reaches his throne. Hegemon passes twice and the rest three times. When they reach a spot Northwest of the Station of Stolistes, Kerux and Neophyte halt.

Hiero: *Take your station Northwest of the Stolistes.*

Kerux motions Neophyte to seat, passing to a place between Pillars and Altar. Hegemon replaces his chair and sits down. Kerux replaces elements on Altar, returning to place (clockwise). All are seated.

Hiero: *The Threefold Cord bound about your waist was the image of the threefold bondage of mortality, which amongst the uninitiated is termed earthly or Material inclination, that has bound into a narrow place the once far-wandering Soul; and the Hoodwink was an image of the darkness, of Ignorance, of Mortality that has blinded men to the happiness and Beauty their eyes once looked upon.*

The Double Cubical Altar in the center of the Hall is an emblem of visible Nature or the Material Universe, concealing within herself the mysteries of all dimensions, while revealing her surface to the exterior senses. It is a double cube because, as the Emerald Tablet has said, "The things that are below are a reflection of the things that are above." The world of men and women created to unhappiness is a reflection of the World of Divine Beings created to Happiness. It is described in the SEPHER YETSIRAH or Book of Formation as "An Abyss of Height" and as an "Abyss of Depth," "An Abyss of the East" and "An Abyss of the West," "An Abyss of the North" and "An Abyss of the South." The Altar is black because, unlike Divine Beings who unfold in the Element of Light, the Fires of Created Beings arise from Darkness and Obscurity.

On the Altar is a White Triangle to be in the image of that Immortal Light, the Triune Light, which moved in darkness and formed the World out of Darkness. There are two contending Forces and one always uniting them. And these Three have their Image in the Threefold Flame of our Being and in the threefold wave of the sensual world.

Hierophant stands in the form of a cross, holding Banner of East.

Glory be to Thee, Father of the undying. For Thy Glory flows out rejoicing to the ends of the Earth.

Reseats himself.

The Red Cross above the White Triangle is an image of Him Who was unfolded in the Light. At its East, South, West, and North Angles are a Rose, Fire, Cup of Wine, and Bread and Salt. These allude to the Four Elements, Air, Fire, Water, Earth. The Mystical Words—KHABS AM PEKHT—are ancient Egyptian, and are the origin of the Greek "KONX OM PAX," which was uttered at the Eleusinian Mysteries. A literal translation would be "Light Rushing Out in One Ray" and they signify the same form of Light as that symbolized by the Staff of the Kerux.

East of the Double Cubical Altar of created things are the Pillars of Hermes and Solomon. On these are painted certain Hieroglyphics from the 17th and 125th Chapters of the Book of the Dead. They are the doorposts of the Gateway of the Hidden Wisdom. They are the symbols of the twin powers of Day and Night, Love and Hate, Work and Rest, the subtle

*force of the Lodestone and the Eternal out-pouring and
in-pouring of the Heart of God. The lamps that burn, though
with a veiled light, upon their summits show that the
Pathway to Hidden Knowledge, unlike the Pathway of
Nature—which is a continual undulation, the winding
hither and thither of the Serpent—is the straight and narrow
way between them.*

*It was because of this that I passed between them, when you
came to the Light, and it was because of this that you were
placed between them to receive the Final Consecration. Two
contending Forces and one which unites them eternally. Two
Basal angles of the triangle and one which forms the apex.
Such is the origin of Creation—it is the Triad of Life.*

*My Throne at the Gate of the East is the place of the
Guardian of the Dawning Sun.*

*The Throne of Hiereus at the Gate of the West is the place of
the Guardian against the Multitudes that sleep through the
Light and awaken at the Twilight.*

*The Throne of the Hegemon seated between the Columns is
the Place of Balanced Power, between the Ultimate Light and
the Ultimate darkness. These meanings are shown in detail
by our insignia and the color of our robes.*

*The Wand of the Kerux is the beam of Light from the
Hidden Wisdom and his Lamp is an emblem of the
ever-burning Lamp of the Guardian of the Mysteries.*

*The Seat of the Stolistes at the Gate of the North is the Place
of the Guardian of the Cauldron and the Well of Water—of
Cold and Moisture.*

*The Seat of the Dadouchos at the Gate of the South is the
Place of the Guardian of the Lake of Fire and the Burning
Bush.*

*Frater Kerux, I command you to declare that the Neophyte
has been initiated into the Mysteries of the 0=0 Grade.*

Kerux advances to right front of Hierophant, raises wand.

Kerux: *In the name of the Lord of the Universe, Who works in
Silence and Whom naught but Silence can express, and by*

command of the Very Honored Hierophant, hear ye all, that I proclaim that _____, who will henceforth be known to you by the motto _____, has been duly admitted to the 0=0 Grade as a Neophyte of the Order of the Stella Matutina.

Kerux returns to place, saluting Hierophant.

Hiero: *Honored Hiereus, I delegate to you the duty of pronouncing a short address to our Frater on his admission.*

Hiereus: *Frater (Soror) _____, it is my duty to deliver this exhortation to you. Remember your Obligation in this Order to secrecy—for Strength is in Silence, and the seed of Wisdom is sown in Silence and grows in Darkness and Mystery.*

Remember that you hold all religions in reverence, for there is none but contains a Ray from the Ineffable Light that you are seeking. Remember the penalty that awaits the breaker of His Oath. Remember the Mystery that you have received, and that the Secret of Wisdom can be discerned only from the place of balanced Powers.

Study well the Great Arcanum of the proper equilibrium of Severity and Mercy, for either unbalanced is not good. Unbalanced Severity is cruelty and oppression; unbalanced Mercy is but weakness and would permit Evil to exist unchecked, thus making itself, as it were, the accomplice of that Evil.

Remember that things Divine are not attained by mortals who understand the Body alone, for only those who are lightly armed can attain the summit.

Remember that God alone is our Light and the Bestower of Perfect Wisdom and that no mortal power can so more than bring you to the Pathway of that Wisdom, which he could, if it so pleased him, put into the heart of a child. For as the whole is greater than the part, so are we but Sparks from the Insupportable Light which is in Him.

The ends of the Earth are swept by the borders of his Garment of Flame—from him all things proceed, and unto Him all things return. Therefore, we invoke Him. Therefore even the Banner of the East falls in adoration before Him.

Hiero: *Before you can ask to pass to a higher Grade, you will have to commit certain rudiments of Occult Knowledge to memory. A manuscript lecture in these subjects will be supplied you by the Chief in whose charge they are. When you can pass an examination in this elementary Qabbalistic Knowledge, you will inform the Member in whose charge you are, and arrangements will be made for you to sit for examination. If you are found perfect, you will then apply for admission to the next Degree. Remember, that without a Dispensation from the Second Order, no person can be admitted or advanced to a Grade of the First Order.*

Kerux conducts Neophyte to his table (going clockwise), gives him a solution, telling him to pour a few drops on the plate before him.

Kerux: *Nature is harmonious in all her workings, and that which is above is as that which is below. Thus also, the Truths which by material Science we investigate, are but special examples of the all-pervading Laws of the Universe. So, within this pure and limpid fluid, lie hidden and unperceived of mortal eyes the elements bearing the semblance of blood, even as within the mind and brain of the initiate lie concealed the Divine Secrets of the Hidden Knowledge. Yet if the Oath be forgotten, and solemn pledge broken, then that which is secret shall be revealed, even as this pure fluid reveals the semblance of blood.*

Kerux pours liquid into plate.

Let this remind thee forever, O Neophyte, how easily by a careless or unthinking word, thou mayest betray that which thou hast sworn to keep secret and mayest reveal the Hidden Knowledge imparted to thee, and implanted in thy brain and in thy mind. And let the hue of blood remind thee that if thou shalt fail in this thy oath of secrecy, thy blood may be poured out and thy body broken, for heavy is the penalty exacted by the Guardians of the Hidden Knowledge from those who wilfully betray their trust.

Cancellarius superintends signing of the Roll.

Hiero: *Resume your seat, and remember that your admission to this Order gives you no right to initiate any other person without Dispensation from the Greatly Honored Chiefs of the Second Order.*

Closing

Hierophant, or any other member by his command, rises to enquire if anyone has anything to propose for the good of the Order for the first, second, and third time. Then may Hierophant address Neophyte.

Kerux passes to Northwest of Hierophant's throne, raising wand.

Kerux: *HEKAS! HEKAS! ESTE BEBELOI!*

Kerux then returns to place (going clockwise) Saluting Throne.

Hiero: *Fratres et Sorores of the Smaragdum Thallasses Temple of the Order of the Stella Matutina, assist me to close the Hall of the Neophyte.*

All rise.

Hiereus: (knocks)

Hegemon: (knocks)

Kerux: (knocks)

Sentinel: (knocks)

Hiero: *Frater Kerux, see that the Hall is properly guarded.*

Kerux: (knocks as in opening) *The Hall is properly guarded, Very Honored Hierophant.*

Hiero: *Honored Hiereus, assure yourself that all present have beheld the Stella Matutina.*

Hiereus: *Fratres et Sorores, give the Signs.*
   Very Honored Hierophant, all present have been so honored.

Hiero: *Let the Hall be purified by Water and Fire.*

Stolistes: (purifies as in Opening) *I purify by Water.*

Dadouchos: (consecrates as in Opening) *I consecrate with Fire.*

Hiero: *Let the Mystical Reverse Circumambulation take place in the Pathway of Light.*

Kerux passes by West to South, Hegemon by North to West and South. Hiereus direct to South, then members. Stolistes by West to South on left of Dadouchos. Kerux leads, all saluting as they pass East—each time. Hiereus falls out when they pass his throne. Hegemon falls out when they pass his throne, Hegemon twice round, the rest three times.

Hiero: *The Mystical Reverse Circumambulation is accomplished. It is the symbol of Fading Light. Let us adore the Lord of the Universe.*

All turn East.

Hiero: *Holy art Thou, Lord of the Universe!* (all salute)
   Holy are Thou, Whom nature hath not formed! (all salute)
   Holy art Thou, the Vast and the Mighty One! (all salute)
   Lord of the Light, and of the Darkness! (Sign of Silence)
   All turn to center and salute as in Opening.

Alternative Adoration
Holy art Thou, Father of Beings and of Spaces.
Holy art Thou, Who didst in reason constitute the things that are.
Holy art Thou, Whom nature hath not Formed.
Holy art Thou, Who workest in Silence and Whom nought but Silence can express.

(Repeat salute at each adoration)

Hiero: *Nothing now remains but to partake together in silence, of the Mystic Repast, composed of the symbols of the Four Elements, and to repeat our pledge of secrecy.*

Kerux lights lamp on altar.

Hierophant quits Throne without scepter or Banner, goes West of Altar, faces East and gives Saluting Sign.

Hiero: *I invite you to inhale with me the perfume of this Rose, as a symbol of Air.*

    To feel the warmth of this sacred Fire. (spreads hands over it)

    To eat with me this Bread and Salt as types of Earth. (breaks and dips bread in salt and eats)

    And finally to drink with me this Wine, the consecrated emblem of Elemental Water.

Drinks from cup after making a Sign of the Cross with it. All subsequently make Sign of Cross with cup before drinking. Hierophant passes to East of Altar (going clockwise) and administers Repast to senior Chief, raising and handling Elements. The saluting Sign (first part), is made by each towards the altar on coming forward, the celebrant replying with the Sign of Silence. The Chiefs in their order partake first, then the Officers (except Kerux), including Sentinel, from Hiereus to Dadouchos.

Hiero: *Let all members below the grade of Portal be seated.*

All 5=6 members then communicate in the order in which they happen to be seated, beginning with the nearest to the left of Hierophant and working round South, West, and East. Each lifts and hands the Elements to the one who comes after him, returning to his place round the Altar (clockwise) and then sits down. When the last 5=6 member is East of Altar:-

Hiero: *Let all members of the 4=7 degree now rise.* (They rise and partake as before)

    Let all members of the 3=8 degree now rise. (They rise and partake as before)

Let all members of the 2=9 degree now rise. (They rise and partake as before)
Let all members of the 1=10 degree now rise. (They rise and partake as before)
Let the Neophytes now rise.

They rise and partake as before; when the last Neophyte is at the Altar the Kerux steps up without insignia and partakes. When the cup is handed to him he finishes the wine and bread and, holding the Cup on high, turns it upside down, crying loudly:—

It is finished.

Kerux returns to his place.
All rise.

Hiero: *TETELESTAI.*

Hiero: (knocks)

Hiereus: (knocks)

Hegemon: (knocks)

Hiero: (knocks) *KHABS.*

Hiereus: (knocks) *AM.*

Hegemon: (knocks) *PEKHT.*

Hiereus: (knocks) *KONX.*

Hegemon: (knocks) *OM.*

Hiero: (knocks) *PAX.*

Hegemon: (knocks) *LIGHT.*

Hiero: (knocks) *IN.*

Hiereus: (knocks) *EXTENSION.*

All make signs towards Altar.

Hiero: *May what we have partaken of sustain us in our search for the QUINTESSENCE, the Stone of the Philosophers, True*

Wisdom, Perfect Happiness, the SUMMUM BONUM.

All disrobe and disperse.

If the Hall is not reserved exclusively for Temple purposes, it should be purified by the lesser Ritual of the Pentagram being performed by the Hierophant with his scepter as soon as the members are assembled.

In case of the Hall not being duly oriented, the following prayer should be said by the Hierophant before the formal opening and after performance of the Lesser Ritual of the Pentagram. The Hierophant face the true East and between that point and the Altar says:—

> *Creator of the Universe, Lord of the Visible World, who hast by Thy Supreme Will set limits to its magnitude and conferred special attributes on its boundaries, we invoke Thee to grant that whatever hidden and mystic virtue doth reside in the radiant East—the Dayspring of Light—the origin of Life—may in answer to this our prayer be this day conferred upon the Throne of the Hierophant of this Temple, who is the emblem of the Dawning of that Golden light which shall illuminate the Path of the Unknown and shall guide us at length to the attainment of the Quintessence, the Stone of the Wise, True Wisdom and Perfect Happiness.*

Part 2
The Commentary

A Commentary on
The Neophyte Ritual

Containing Z.1, Z.2, and Additional Material

Application to Join a Temple

The following is an example of a request to join a Golden Dawn
Temple. All applicants are expected to sign and return the form
(taken from an early Golden Dawn document) for consideration
of their eligibility to join the Temple.

Some years since, permission was granted by the Secret
Chiefs of the Order to certain Fratres learned in the Occult
Sciences to direct the Working of the Esoteric Order of the
G.˙.D.˙. in the Outer, with the view of aiding the study of
Occultism and the mysteries of Life and Death; further also
authorizing them to hold meetings both for the purposes of
Study and also for the Initiation and Advancement of any
person of either Sex, who should be accepted as a candidate by
the Chiefs and who should be prepared and willing to take an
Obligation of the most solemn character to maintain Absolute
Secrecy regarding all things to the Order (such Obligation
being nowise contrary to either their Civil, Moral, or Religious
duties).

Belief in a Supreme Being, or Beings, is indispensable. In
addition, the candidate, if not a Christian, should be at least
prepared to take on an interest in Christian Symbolism.

The Chiefs of the Order do not care to accept as Candidates
any persons accustomed to submit[ting] themselves as Medi-

ums to the Experiments of Hypnotism, Mesmerism, or Spiritualism; or who habitually allow themselves to fall into a completely passive condition of will; also they disapprove of the methods made use of as a rule in such Experiments.

This Order is not established for the benefit of those who desire merely a superficial knowledge of Occult Science:

Preliminary Pledge to be Signed by Intending Candidate
I the undersigned do hereby solemnly pledge myself:

(1) That I am over the age of 21 years.

(2) That I join this Order of my own free Will and accord.

(3) To keep secret this Order, its Name, its members, and its Proceedings, from every person outside its pale; and even from Initiates unless in actual possession of the Pass-Word for the time being. I further promise to keep secret any information relative to this Order which may become known to me before my admission; and I also pledge myself to divulge nothing whatsoever to the outside World concerning this Order in case [of] either my Resignation, Demission or Expulsion therefrom.

(4) Undertake to prosecute with zeal the study of Occult Sciences.

(5) If accepted as a candidate, I undertake to persevere through the Ceremony of Admission.

(Signature in Full) _____

Dated this _____ day of _____, 19___

I select the following for my Motto: _____

(Latin is preferable)

I desire that communications may be addressed to me as under:

(Address in Full): _____

Acceptance of a Candidate

The acceptance of a Candidate for a Golden Dawn, A.O., or Stella Matutina varied to a certain degree. Wherever possible, the candidate was first interviewed by a panel of members. This was followed by an "Astral Investigation," which was performed by a clairvoyant member of the Temple. Usually, this person was one of the Chiefs, or a person sufficiently high enough in the Order and nominated by the Chiefs, to astrally investigate the candidate.

During the later years of the Stella Matutina, this practice fell into abeyance. A good documented example of this is shown in *The Sword of Wisdom,* where Ithell Colquhoun tried to become a member of an A.O. temple (which I assume was in the early 1930s) under the Chieftainship of Mrs. Weir. A few nights after applying to join the temple, Colquhoun underwent an experience that she termed an "invasion" where she experienced an impersonal force coming into contact with her and which she termed the "Power of the Y." After this experience, she was refused membership to the A.O. Temple.

To most people who understand any type of psychic activity, this is relatively straightforward enough. Consider the psychic experiments allegedly undertaken by the C.I.A., where those that were psychic enough drew maps of secret missile installations in Russia. It would be fair comment to say that if one has the psychic ability, he or she can drop in and investigate anybody. The exception to this is a trained Adept who has the ability to recognize and neutralize this force (though we doubt the C.I.A. has studied this type of research). Colquhoun also mentioned that this force may have been the "Secret Chiefs" (as opposed to the elderly matrons who took the office of Chiefs at the time).

It has been our experience that not one but two types of psychic investigations can take place. The first, an investigation by an Order clairvoyant, cannot always be deemed accurate unless it is done by someone who has a proven ability in that field. The second is when people who have applied to join the Order experience the same symptoms quoted by Colquhoun. This must be done on an entirely involuntary basis. It has been described as a cloud or energy field descending on one. By "involuntary," we mean that it was not done on any conscious level by any temple officer. The latter form of investigation has been noted more than once at Whare Ra, and also by a number of initiates of our Thoth-Hermes Temple. Whether it is an effect of the "Secret Chiefs" or not, we cannot say; but, according to what we have seen, this type of investigation generally occurs to people who are deemed unqualified to advance far into the Order and, in the view of hindsight, would generally be considered unsuitable as Second Order material.

Most people may wonder why, if this type of examination of candidates was available, did the Golden Dawn undergo so much turmoil? The answer is simple enough. This type of investigation can only be applied to the Outer Order (for reasons mentioned above) where people are not in a position to dictate terms to the Inner Order. Jack Taylor pointed out to us a number of cases at Whare Ra where some members were perfect Outer Order members and put all their efforts behind the Order. But once admitted to the Inner Order, things changed to the opposite. We know of one American Temple Chief, a trained psychologist, who uses her training and her ability to be able to read the horoscopes of prospective members to see if they are suitable before they are admitted. However, going on the track record of this temple, from those who have left it, this method is not any more successful than the astral examinations of the earlier temples.

Preparation of the Candidate

The preparation of the Candidate differed to a certain extent from temple to temple within the Golden Dawn, and later in the Stella Matutina. The following description is an example of what is undergone in the New Zealand Order.

Once it is decided that a Candidate is suitable for initiation by the Chiefs, the Hierophant then obtains a natal birth chart from the aspirant. From this, an electional chart is made up. The two are joined together so that a suitable time for the ritual can be worked out.

Once this is done, a temple member, or one of the temple officers of the oncoming ceremony, instructs the Candidate to:

(1) Fast at least four hours before the ritual. This is done to ensure an empty stomach, which makes the psychic channels more open and receptive to stimulation.

(2) Bathe in herbs of the lilacae family, which relate to Malkuth. These herbs penetrate the aura and leave a residue in it that makes it receptive to the auric manipulation which is conducted during the ceremony.

(3) Meditate on a suitable name for at least twenty minutes before the ceremony. Generally this form of meditation uses the Hebrew name of the Order (ChBRH ZRCh BQR AWR—Society of the Shining Light of Dawn), which the Candidate is told to repeat

continuously until s/he is blindfolded by the Sentinel. The theory behind this meditation is that constant repetition of the name, by the aspirant, helps break down the astral sheaths between him/herself and the Order.

Preparation of the Hall

The temple layout is shown in Figure 1. The first officer to enter the Hall before the ceremony is the Kerux, whose duties are to set up the temple furniture. This officer is followed by the Stolistes, who attends to the placing of the Holy Water and oversees that all robes and insignias are ready. (Temples like Whare Ra usually supplied the robes, but, in smaller temples, the individual officers generally had their own. Regardless, it is still the duty of the Stolistes to check with each member to be sure that everything is in order.) The Dadouchos is the last of the junior officers to enter the temple. It is his or her duty to attend to the lamps, censers, and candles.

Once all the physical temple props are in place, the officers vacate the temple about one hour before the start of the ceremony so that the Hierophant can enter. It is s/he who must create the astral shells of the various god-forms and energize them according to the temple floor plan, as shown in Figure 2. This is done with each god-form on an individual basis. It is extremely important that each astral shell be in its correct size, shape, and color. These are brought as close to the stage of manifestation as possible by the Hierophant. S/he will, through his/her own aura, know exactly how far to activate them. This would still be considered on a low vibrational scale. It is accomplished through the use of the DWB (Divine White Brilliance) or LVX formula, as it is sometimes called, which links together the Nephesch and the Ruach of the Hierophant. The shells of these god-forms are, at this point, linked to the Ruach of the Hierophant. They can be considered as a type of blind force at a low vibrational pitch. They are, in fact, not fully activated and could be described as the Nephesch of themselves.

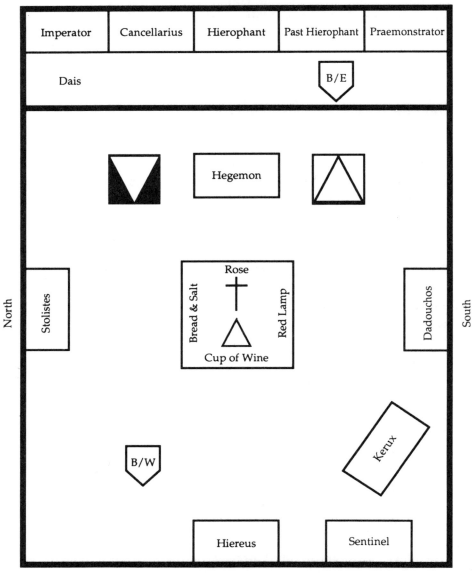

Figure 1
Temple Layout

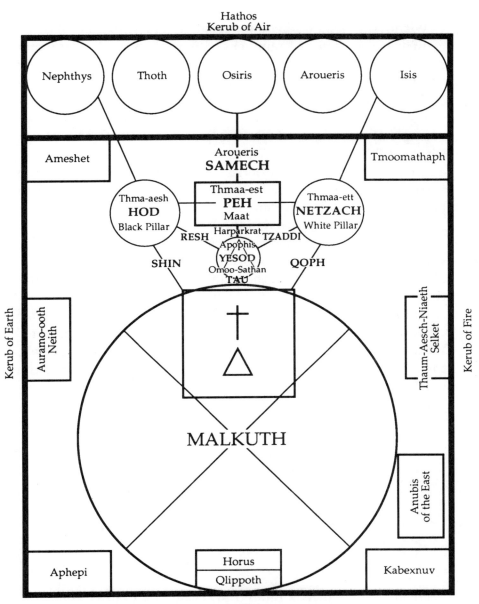

Figure 2
Temple Layout Showing Location of God-Forms

Within the Golden Dawn, the creation and utilization of these god-forms was done at a number of different levels, and for many different reasons. Their use in rituals like the 0=0 is mainly two-fold. The first is the building up of the god-form so that you can link your energy to it, so that you can draw from its power by complete identification and absorption of its qualities. An example of this is given by Israel Regardie in his Golden Dawn Ritual of Transformation. Within the 0=0, another aspect is then approached with the formation of more than one god-form in the astral so that each force will counterbalance the other. The formula by which this is done is:

(1) The Banishing Ritual of the Pentagram.

(2) By AHIH (bring down the power) to the Tiphareth center where the names of the god-forms are formulated in white.

(3) Vibratory formula of the name of each god-form—as many times as there are letters in their names .

(4) Project the rose ray into the astral and then create them.

The colors of these temple god-forms are extremely important. While the power of the Ruach initially forms their Astral Shell, their flashing colors are needed to attract the power that the god-form represents. The Mathers papers on "Telesmatic Images" explains how this is done:

> Now there is also a mode whereby, combining the letters, the colours, the attributions and their Synthesis, thou mayest build up a telesmatic Image of a Force. The Sigil shall then serve thee for the tracing of a Current which shall call into action a certain Elemental Force. And know thou that this is not to be done lightly for thine amusement or experiment, seeing that the Forces of Nature were not created to be thy plaything or toy. Unless thou doest thy practical magical works with solemnity, ceremony and reverence, thou shalt be like an infant playing with fire . . .

Though this paper is related to telesmatic figures, the same fundamental principles of formulation in the astral still apply. The sigils referred to here are the ones traced from the rose cross (see Golden Dawn Flying Rolls 2 and 6 for correct use of this method). [These documents can be found in *Astral Projection, Ritual Magic, and Alchemy*, edited by Francis King, Rochester, VT: Destiny Books, 1987.—*Eds.*]

In general the ray with the name projected from the Tiphareth center will perform much the same function. This whole procedure can be quite exhausting and is generally done from a paper, with names, colors, and sigils of the Invisible Stations used as a prompt. In his book *Energy, Prayer, and Relexation*, Regardie says,

> The ancient custom was to image the form of the God, a fairly common pictograph, and whilst uttering the prayer to feel that this god-form enveloped the body of the invoker.

This is, of course, another method of creating the astral shell of the god-form by the use of prayer. The first method, quoted above, was the one taught to Taylor, who was a stickler that one must always have the form on paper, in front of one, before the invocations are begun. Though Hierophants are expected to know every shape and position of a god-form by heart, the god-form formulation is generally done from a temple diagram so that no mistakes can be made.

The robes of the officers also play an important part. When the astral shells of the god-form are created, they are linked to the robes and badges of the officers who are placed in the positions they occupy around the Hall. Once the Hierophant has completed this task (which can take from 30 to 40 minutes to perform correctly) the Dadouchos is then brought back into the temple and performs the candle-lighting ceremony, watched by the (throned) Hierophant. It is important to remember that a candle is placed in the quarter it represents. The Yellow candle for the East, however, is placed between the pillars and slightly behind the chair of the Hegemon.

The ceremony of candle lighting is always started at the East, going in a clockwise spiral, until the final candle on the altar is lit. Two main things occur during this exercise. The first is that the Hierophant extends his/her Ruach to the fire of the Dadouchos. The second is that the aura of the Dadouchos gives the flame its link which, controlled by the Hierophant, brings the first active element into the floor plan, for Fire is the first manifested element.

During this ceremony, the Hierophant must have the ability to "cradle the aura of the Dadouchos." By this I mean s/he must reach out and control the actions of the Dadouchos on the Astral through a process of auric manipulation. (This is later manipulated by the Hegemon.)

After this, the rest of the Temple officers are admitted. They go to their respective stations and await the Kerux, the final officer to enter the Hall, after s/he has attended to the Candidate.

At this point, we should mention that, in the Golden Dawn and the early stages of the Stella Matutina, the temple officers on the floor could be Outer Order Grades. However, the 78 additional years of ritual of the Stella Matutina have shown that the energy fields that these junior officers have to work with are much more complex than was first thought.

In the later years of the Stella Matutina and the Smaragdum Thalasses, here in New Zealand, it was thought that these floor officers should all be Inner Group members, where possible. Prior to his or her entrance to the Temple, all officers would sit quietly in order to link their Ruachs and Neshamahs (which under normal circumstances cannot be done by Outer Order members). Hence, their activated Spheres of Sensations (auras) then link into, and feed, the astral shells of the Invisible Stations created by the Hierophant. This also, to a certain extent, gives the Hierophant an element of control over the stations linked to each officer. S/he can, in fact, control the link by increasing, or decreasing, the vibrational pitch of the god-form, where there is an excess or decrease of energy. This can be brought about by the mood of the temple officer in order to balance things together in the overall floorplan.

When these officers take their positions and link their Ruachs with the Nephesch of the form created by the Hierophant, it is important that they have a correct mental image of the god-form they are assuming. This is, in fact, god-form assumption in a group format. The officers on the Dais also have a part to play in this preparation. They usually enter, with the rest of the officers, after the candles are lit by the Dadouchos. Once seated on their respective Thrones, they also link their Ruachs with the Nephesch shells created by the Hierophant. The following paper outlines the coloring and positioning of each of the astral shells that the Hierophant has to create around the temple before the start of the ceremony. It is more complete than previously published papers, in the sense that additional notes have been added to explain the reasons why some of the god-forms are colored the way they are.

The Egyptian God-Forms of the Neophyte Grade

The stations of the god-forms used in our symbolism come under two heads:

1. Visible Stations.
2. Invisible Stations.

The Visible Stations are the places of the officers, each of whom has a special astral shape suitable to the forces s/he represents. On the Dais are places for the Three Chiefs, the Past Hierophant, and the current Hierophant. The order in which they sit (as you face East, from left to right) is:

Imperator—Nepthys
Cancellarius—Thoth
Hierophant—Osiris
Past Hierophant—Aroueris
Praemonstrator—Isis

The names below are those of the god-forms they represent. The following are descriptions of the god-forms of the seven officers of the Neophyte Grade.

Hierophant: Osiris in the netherland. Expounder of the mysteries in the Hall of the Dual Manifestation of the Goddess of Truth. The Hierophant is represented by two god-forms, the passive and the active aspects of Osiris, as shown in Figures 3 and 4. Seated on the Dais, as Hierophant, he is clothed in the god-form of Osiris. As Osiris, he wears the tall White Crown of the South, flanked by feathers stripped white and blue. His face

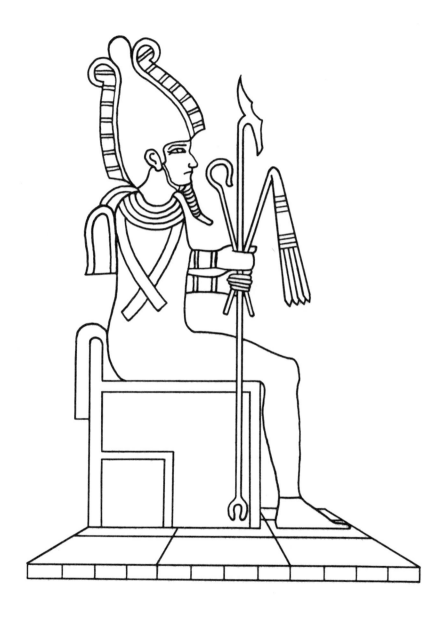

Figure 3
Osiris

Figure 4
Aroueris

is green, his eyes blue. From his chin hangs the royal beard of authority and judgement, blue in color and gold tipped. He wears a collar in bands of red, blue, yellow, and black. On his back is a bundle, strapped across his chest by scarlet bands. He is in mummy wrappings to the feet. His hands are free to hold a golden Phoenix Wand, a Blue Crook, and Red Scourge. His hands are green. His feet rest on a pavement of black and white.

The colors used to construct this figure are a mixture of Golden Dawn teachings and the traditional colors of the figure. As an example, the blue and white crown and blue beard show both the influence of Kether and the Path of Samekh, while the yellow tip shows the Air element. The bands of his collar represent the four elements, while the scarlet bands across him allude to the Rosicrucian grade. The Phoenix Wand is traditional, while its golden color shows that it comes through Tiphareth. The green skin coloring is from the traditional coloring. The blue crook and red scourge shows that he holds together both the power of Geburah and Chesed.

Although no official paper was ever issued on the subject of the Egyptian god-form coloring, Jack Taylor said that Felkin's master copy, from the old Order, was often consulted during the 0=0 discussions. This was Westcott's copy which was destroyed when Whare Ra closed. To the best of my knowledge, no other copy of this document exists in the New Zealand Order.

The god-form of Osiris never moves from the Dais. When the Hierophant has to move from the Dais, s/he is covered in the form of Osiris in action—Aroueris, which is built up by the Past Hierophant, seated on the Hierophant's left. If no one is seated as past Hierophant, then Inner Members help the Hierophant to formulate the second god-form.

Aroueris, or Horus the Elder, is very lively to look upon—like pure flames. He wears a Double Crown of Egypt, the cone-shaped crown in red inside the White Crown of the North, with a white plume. His nemyss is purple banded with gold at the edges. His face and body are translucent scarlet. He has green eyes and wears the purple beard of authority. He wears a yellow tunic with a waistcloth of yellow striped with purple, from which depends a lion's tail. In common with all Egyptian Gods, he has a white linen kilt showing like an apron under the colored waistcloth. His armlets and anklets are of gold. He carries in his right hand a blue Phoenix Wand and in his left a blue Ankh. He stands on a pavement of purple and gold.

Hiereus: Horus in the abode of Blindness unto and Ignorance of the Higher Avenger of the Gods (see Figure 5).

He wears the Double Crown of the South and North, red and white, over a nemyss of scarlet banded with emerald green. His face is that of a lively hawk—tawny and black with bright, piercing eyes; his throat is white. His body, like that of Aroueris, is entirely scarlet. He wears a collar, armlets, and anklets of emerald; a waistcloth of emerald stripped red, from which depends a lion's tail, and he carries in his right hand an Emerald Phoenix Wand and in his left a Blue Ankh. He stands on a pavement of emerald and scarlet.

Hegemon: Thmaa-Est "Before the Face of the Gods in the place of the Threshold."

Thmaa-est wears a black nemyss bound at the brow with a purple band from which rises, in front, a tall ostrich feather of green striped with red in equal bands. (A version of this goddess is shown in Figure 6.) She wears a banded collar of red, yellow, blue, and black. Her tunic is emerald green to the feet, where it is banded to match the collar. She has purple and green shoulder straps and a purple girdle also bordered in the colors mentioned above. Her face and body are natural color—i.e., a light Egyptian red-brown. She wears armlets of emerald and red and carries a combined form of Lotus and Phoenix Wand. It has an orange flower and a blue stem and ends in an orange Sign of the Binary. In her left hand, she carries a blue Ankh, and she stands on a pavement of yellow and purple bordered with blocks of red, blue, yellow, and black, in succession.

Kerux: Anubis of the East as shown in Figure 7. Watcher of the Gods.

Figure 5
Horus

Figure 6
Thmaa–Est

Anubis has the head of a black jackal, very alert, pointed ears well pricked up. His nemyss is purple banded with white; he wears a collar of yellow and purple bands and a tunic of yellow flecked with tufts of black hair. His body is red. His waistcloth is yellow striped with purple, and from it hangs a lion's tail. His ornaments are purple and gold; his Phoenix Wand and Ankh are blue. He stands on a pavement of purple and yellow.

Stolistes: Auramo-ooth. "The Light shining through the Waters upon Earth" "Goddess of the Scales of the Balance at the Black Pillar"

Auramo-ooth is mainly in blue. Her face and body are natural. (A version of this god-form is shown in Figure 8.) She wears a blue Crown of the North from which springs a delicate gold plume over a vulture headdress of orange and blue. Her collar is orange and blue, she carries a blue Ankh and a Lotus Wand, having an orange lotus on a green stem. Her plain blue tunic reaches to the feet. She stands on black.

Dadouchos: Thaum-Aesch-Niaeth. "Perfection through Fire manifesting on Earth" "Goddess of the Scales of the Balance at the White Pillar"

Thaum-aesch is mainly in red. Her face and body are natural. (A version of this god-form is shown in Figure 9.) She wears a red Crown of the South flanked by two feathers in green barred black over a vulture headdress in red and green. Her collar is red and green, and she carries a green Ankh and a Lotus Wand with a red flower and green stem. Her simple red tunic reaches to her feet and she stands on black.

Sentinel: Anubis of the West.

His form is the same as that of Kerux, but his nemyss, ornaments, and dress are black and white. He has a lion's tail and carries a black Phoenix Wand and Ankh. He stands on black. Anubis of the West is shown in Figure 10.

Figure 7
Anubis of the East

Figure 8
Auramo-Ooth

Figure 9
Thaum-Aesch-Niaeth

Figure 10
Anubis of the West

The Three Chiefs

Imperator: Nephthys

Nephthys has a face and body of translucent gold (see Figure 11). She is crowned with a cap over a vulture headdress of black and white, the vulture head being red. Her collar and ornaments are black and white, and she wears a black robe to the feet. It is bordered in black and white. She carries a blue Ankh and a Lotus Wand with a green flower and blue stem. She stands on black and white pavement.

Praemonstrator: Isis

Isis has a face and body of translucent gold (see Figure 12). She is crowned with a throne over a vulture headdress of blue and orange. The vulture head is red. Her robe is of blue bordered with gold. Her ornaments are blue and orange, and she carries a blue Ankh and Lotus Wand with a green flower and blue stem. She stands on blue and orange.

Cancellarius: Tho-oth

The god-form of Thoth is built up by the Cancellarius or the officer seated on the right of the Hierophant. This is his Visible Station; but, during a Neophyte Grade, he also has an Invisible Station in the East while the Obligation takes place.

He has an Ibis head, black beak, and white throat (see Figure 13). His nemyss is yellow bordered with mauve. His collar is yellow with a middle band of squares in mauve and green. His tunic is mauve with yellow stripes, and he has a lion's tail. His limbs are natural color; his ornaments are red and green. He carries a blue Ankh and a stylus and writing tablet. He stands on mauve and yellow.

The Invisible Stations

These fall naturally into four groups given below in their order of importance.

1. Stations in the Path Samekh in the Middle Pillar—Hathor, Harparkraat, Evil persona.

Figure 11
Nephthys

Figure 12
Isis

Figure 13
Thoth

2. Kerubim
3. Children of Horus
4. The Forty-Two Assessors

1. *Hathor:* This Great Goddess formulates behind the Hierophant in the East (see Figure 14). Her face and limbs are of
translucent gold. She wears a scarlet Sun Disc resting between
black horns from the back of which rise two feathers in white,
barred blue. She has a black nemyss. The colors of her collar
follow the pattern of blue, red, and blue. Blue bands support her
robe of orange, which is bordered with blue and red. Her ornaments are blue and orange. She carries a blue Ankh and a Lotus
Wand with a green flower and a blue stem. She stands on black
bordered with blue.

Harparkraat: He formulates in the center of the Hall between
Hegemon and the Altar, where he sits or stands on a Lotus facing
East (see Figure 15). His face and body are translucent emerald
green. He has blue eyes and a curl of blue hair, denoting youth,
comes round his face on the right side. He wears the double
crown, red and white. His collar is yellow and blue; his waistcloth
is yellow and blue with a mauve girdle, whence depends a lion's
tail. His Lotus has leaves alternately blue and yellow and rests
on a pavement of mauve and orange. He has no insignia. His left
forefinger is on his lips.

Omoo-Sathan. Typhon, Apophis, Set: The Evil Persona is a
composite figure of the powers arising from the Qlippoth (see
Figure 16). It rises from the base of the altar standing east of the
altar facing West, in the Sign of Typhon. He is black and has an
animal, somewhat lizard-like head and a black body and tail. He
stands on black. His nemyss is of olive green decorated with
russet, his collar of russet and citrine. He has a white apron and
waistcloth of dull red striped with russet. He has no ornaments.

2. *The Kerubim.*
The Kerub of Air is formed behind Hathor, and she is a power
of Hathor and has the same general coloring (see Figure 17). She

Figure 14
Hathor

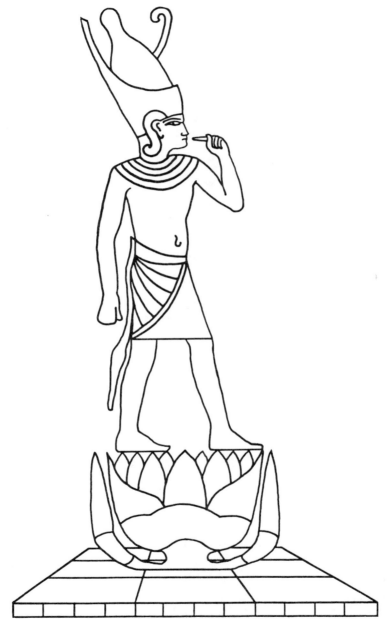

Figure 15
Harparkraat

Figure 16
Omoo-Sathan

has a young girl's countenance and behind her are spread large
and shadowing wings.

The Kerub of Fire is in the South beyond the seat of Dadouchos
(see Figure 18). It is a power of the Great Goddess Tharpesch,
and has the face and form of a Lion with large and clashing
wings. The coloring is very lively and flashing green with ruby
and flame blue and emerald green

Figure 17
Kerub of Air

Figure 18
Kerub of Fire

The Kerub of Water is formed behind Hiereus and is the power of the Great God Toum or Tmu (see Figure 19). It has the face and form of a great Eagle with large and glistening wings. The colors are mostly blue and orange with some green.

The Kerub of Earth is in the North behind the seat of Stolistes (see Figure 20). It is a power of the Great God Ahapshi and has the face and form of a Bull with heavy darkening wings, and the colors are black, green, red with some white.

These forms are not described in detail. We are to imagine them as great stabilizing forces whose forms vary according to circumstances.

3. *Children of Horus.*

These have their invisible stations in the corners of the Hall. They are the guardians of the viscera of the human being—every part of whom comes up for judgment in its right time and place.

Ameshet: The man-faced god is in the Northeast. He has a blue nemyss banded with red, blue, and black. His face is red and has a black ceremonial beard. Round the shoulders of his white mummy shape are bands of red, blue, and black, three times repeated. He stands on red, blue, and black with a border of green, white, and yellow. He is shown in Figure 21.

Tmooathpah: The jackal-headed god is in the Southeast. He has a black face with yellow linings to his pointed ears. He wears a blue nemyss with borders of black, yellow, and blue—the same colors appearing threefold at his shoulders. He has a white mummy shape and stands on blue, yellow and black with a border of green, yellow, and mauve. He is shown in Figure 22.

Kabexnuv: The hawk-faced god is in the Northwest. He has a black, tawny face and a nemyss of black bordered with red, yellow, and black. The same colors appear threefold at his shoulders. He has a white mummy shape and stands on red, yellow, and black with a border of green, mauve, and white. He is shown in Figure 23.

Figure 19
Kerub of Water

Figure 20
Kerub of Earth

Figure 21
Ameshet

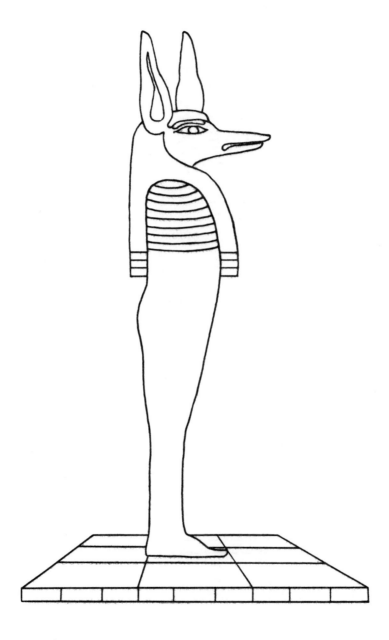

Figure 22
Tmooathpah

Figure 23
Kabexnuv

Aphepi: The ape-faced god is in the Southwest. He has a blue nemyss bordered with red, blue, and yellow bands. These colors appear on his shoulders in the same order. His face is red, and he stands on red, blue, and yellow with a border of green, orange, and mauve. He is shown in Figure 24.

Note: Tmoomathaph is sometimes written Duamutef. Kabexnuv is sometimes written Qebhesenef. Aphepi is sometimes written Mestri or Hapi, while Ameshet is sometimes written Mesti.

4. *The Forty-Two Assessors.* These are not described at all save to say that they make the sign of the Enterer as the Candidate is passed by. They are Witnesses in the Judgment Hall of Osiris.

Note: Clairvoyant members of the Order have shown that the 42 Assessors are placed along the Path of Samekh and above the station of the evil triad. They are back to back and form a length of 21 members. Their descriptions vary, but they are often seen with a variety of animal heads, holding upraised swords. Though placed along this Path, they are far from stationary and rotate slowly, but there are always two lines of 21. Their actual function in the ritual is to create a vortex in various parts of the ceremony that enables them to directly judge the Candidate and his/her Higher Self. (They are placed not at floor level, but at a point just above the height of the Pillars.) This vortex helps keep the Higher Self safe once it has left the body of the Candidate. They also ensure that he/she is judged correctly and they bring to the ceremony a power which is very much like that of the Canopic Gods, only far more detailed. It is their function to examine the Candidate further and test him/her deeper and longer than the length of the ceremony. The 42 Assessors are said to follow and watch the Candidate as he or she goes through each grade and, if found wanting, they will immediately sever his or her link with the Order with the swords they hold. In theory, they remain with the Candidate until admittance to the Inner Order, and it is they who are sometimes responsible for people who leave the Outer Order, barring their admittance to the Inner Order. Each Assessor is related to each letter of the 42 lettered name of God

Figure 24
Aphepi

(which, according to an unpublished Golden Dawn manuscript by Westcott, relates to the Notariqon of the 42 virtues from the 3 consonants of YHVH spelled out) which governs a certain portion of man. The following table, related to the Sephiroth, is the Regardie association of psychological complexes to the Kabbalah.

The Forty-Two Assessors

Name of God	Sephiroth	Part Affected	Assessors
AB	Kether	Id	1. Usekh-nemtet
			2. Hept-seshet
GY	Chokmah	Animus	3. Fenti
			4. Am-khaibitu
ThTz	Binah	Anima	5. Neha-hra
			6. Restau
QROShMN	Chesed	Conscious Ego	7. Maata-f-em-seshet (memory)
			8. Neba
			9. Set-qesu
			10. Khemi
			11. Uatch-nesert
			12. Hra-f-ha-f
KGDYSh	Geburah	Conscious Ego	13. Qerti (will)
			14. Ta-ret
			15. Hetch-abehu
			16. Am-senef
			17. Am-besek
			18. Neb-Maat
BMRTThG	Tiphareth	Conscious Ego	19. Thenemi (imagination)
			20. Anti
			21. Tututef
			22. Uamemti
			23. Maa-ant-f
			24. Her-seru
HQMMNO	Netzach	Conscious Ego	25. Neb-Sekhem (desire)
			26. Seshet-kheru
			27. Nekhen
			28. Kenemti
			29. Kenemti (?)

The Forty-Two Assessors (cont'd.)

Name of God	Sephiroth	Part Affected	Assessors
YGLPZQ	Hod	Conscious Ego	30. Ser-kheru 31. Neb-hrau (reason) 32. Serekhi 33. Neb-abu 34. Nefer-Tem
ShQY	Yesod	Endopsychic	37. Ahi Structure 38. Uatch-rekhit 39. Neheb-nefert
OYTh	Malkuth	Sense Organs	40. Neheb-kau 41. Tcheser-tep 42. An-a-f

Symbolism of the Temple

The Hall of the Neophytes is called "The Hall of the Dual Manifestation of Truth"; that is, "The Hall of the Goddess Thmaah." Her name has three forms, according to the nature of her operation. (See Figure 2 for these three forms in the place of Hegemon.) This is based on Chapters from the Egyptian *Book of the Dead,* modified for Golden Dawn usage.

The second set of major symbolism in the 0=0 blueprint is Kabbalistic and considers an arrangement in the manner of the Sephiroth. The Temple is placed looking towards the YH of YHVH in Malkuth of Assiah. (Y and H answer to the Sephiroth of Chokmah and Binah on the Tree of Life and also to Abba and Aima, through whose knowledge Kether may be obtained.) The Sacred Rites of the Temple should gradually lead the Neophyte into the knowledge of his or her Higher Self. Like the other Sephiroth, Malkuth has also its subsidiary Sephiroth and Paths. Of these ten Sephiroth, the Temple, as arranged in the Neophyte Grade, includes only the lower Sephiroth on the Tree of Life; viz., Malkuth, Yesod, Hod, Netzach, and the outer side of Paroketh, the Veil. Paroketh forms the East of the Temple. The symbolism of the East is of primary importance here.

The bases of the two Pillars are respectively placed in Netzach and Hod; the White Pillar is in Netzach; the Black Pillar is in Hod. They represent the Two Pillars of Mercy and Severity. The bases are cubical and black to represent the Earth element in

73

Malkuth. The columns are respectively black and white to represent the manifestation of the eternal balance of the Scales of Justice. Upon them should be represented, in counter-changed color, any appropriate Egyptian designs emblematic of the soul (see Chapter 3 for a full discussion of this).

The scarlet tetrahedronal capitals represent the Fire of Test and Trial. Between the Pillars is the porchway of the Region Immeasurable. The twin lights which burn on their summits are "The Declarers of the Eternal Truth." The bases of the tetrahedra are triangular. The base of the White Pillar points East, while that of the Black Pillar points West. They thus complete the hexagram of Tiphareth—though separate, as is fitting in "The Hall of the Dual Manifestation of Truth."

The Altar, whose form is that of a double cube, is placed in the eastern part of Malkuth—as far as the Neophyte is concerned. But to the Adeptus Minor, its blackness will veil on the East citrine, on the South olive, and on the North russet, while the West side and the base will be black and the summit is a Brilliant Whiteness.

The symbols on the Altar represent the Forces and the manifestation of the Divine Light. These are concentrated in the White Triangle of the Three Supernals as the synthesis. Upon this sacred and sublime Symbol, the Obligation of the Neophyte is taken. It calls to witness the Forces of the Divine Light.

The Red Cross of Tiphareth (to which the Grade of 5=6 is referred) is placed above the White Triangle, not as dominating it, but as bringing it down and manifesting it unto the Outer Order. It is as though the Crucified One, having raised the symbol of self-sacrifice, had thus touched and brought into action in matter the Divine Triad of Light.

Around the Cross are the symbols of the Four Letters of the Name Jehovah—the Shin of Yeheshuah being only implied and not expressed in the Outer Order. At the East is the Mystical Rose, allied by its scent to the element Air. At the South is the Red Lamp, allied by its Flame with the Element of Fire. At the West is the Cup of Wine, allied by its fluid form to the Element of Water. At the North are Bread and Salt, allied by their substance to the Element of Earth.

The Elements are placed on the Altar according to the Four Winds.

For Osiris on-Nophiris, who is found perfect before the Gods, hath said:

> These are Elements of my Body,
> Perfected through Suffering, Glorified through Trial.
> For the scent of the Dying Rose is as the repressed sigh of my suffering:
> And the flame-red Fire as the Energy of mine Undaunted Will:
> And the Cup of Wine is the pouring out of the Blood of my Heart:
> Sacrificed unto Regeneration, unto the Newer Life:
> And the bread and Salt are as the Foundations of my Body,
> Which I destroy in order that they may be renewed.
> For I am Osiris Triumphant, even Osiris on-Nophris, the Justified:
> I am He who is clothed with the Body of Flesh,
> Yet in whom is the Spirit of the Great Gods:
> I am the Lord of Life, triumphant over Death.
> He who partaketh with me shall arise with me:
> I am the Manifestor in Matter of Those Whose Abode is in the Invisible:
> I am purified: I stand upon the Universe:
> I am its Reconciler with the Eternal Gods:
> I am the Perfector of Matter:
> And without me, the Universe is not.

Technically, the Door of the Hall is supposed to be situated behind the seat of the Hiereus in the West. However, it may be in any part of the Hall, seeing that the walls represent the barrier to the exterior. But this is not always the case, for the barrier is also called the Portal and can be situated within the Hall, usually shaped in an oval fashion.

The corners of the Hall, which are deemed as exterior to the Portal and still within the confines of the Four Children of Horus, are the places where all members of the Temple who wish to view the ceremony are located. They may partake in the circumambulation and, partaking of the Eucharist, they may sit [the seats are in the northwest (0=0), northeast (1=10), west (2=9), southwest (3=8), and northwest (4=7); no seating is behind the Dais for Outer Order members, but those of the Inner Order can be seated there]. When the Hall is small, then the Portal may exceed to the physical barriers of the walls. "The Gate of the Declarers of Judgment" is the name of the Door—its symbolic form is that of a straight and narrow doorway, between the two Mighty Pylons. "The Watcher against the Evil Ones" is the name of the Sentinel who guards, and his/her form is the symbolic one of Anubis.

The Stations, Descriptions and Meanings of the Officers

Hierophant

The Hierophant is placed in the East of the Temple, on the outer side of the Veil of Paroketh (shown in the ritual as a transparent curtain) to rule under the presidency of the Chiefs. S/he is placed in the East because that is where the Sun, ruler of Life, rises. From this position, s/he governs the Hall. In the ancient Mysteries, he was the officer who taught the Rites of Sacrifice and Worship, and he was the Chief Initiating Priest at Eleusis and the equivalent to the Roman *Pontifes Maximum,* or High Priest. The word *hierophantos* is derived from *hieros* and *phaino,* which means "to show forth," "expound," or "teach." He was the head of the ancient Eleusian cult and chosen for life from the hieratic family of the Eumolpidae. Since he was the expounder of the Mysteries, it was necessary that a man of impressive voice should be chosen. This was an office of great responsibility. It is on record that any ancient Hierophant who had publicly shown himself in his ceremonial robes suffered death as a penalty for his indiscretion.

The Hierophant fills the place of a Lord of the Paths of the Portal of the Vault of the Adepts, acting as inductor to the Sacred Mysteries. The Insignia and symbols of the Hierophant are:

(1) The Throne of the East in the Path of Samekh, outside the Veil.

(2) The mantle of bright flame scarlet, bearing a white cross on the left breast and the Robe of Scarlet.

(3) The lamen suspended from a white collar.

(4) The Scepter of Power.

(5) The Banner of the East.

(6) The scarlet-and-white-striped nemyss.

Figure 25
The Mantle or Robe of the Hierophant

The position of the throne on the Path of Samekh is fitting for the Inductor to the Mysteries. It is placed in that balanced and central position of that Path by which alone is safe entrance to the mystical knowledge of the Light in Tiphareth. It is placed before Paroketh at the point of its rending. There it marks the shining forth of the Light through the Veil. The translation of the Three Supernals to the Outer Order is represented by the Red Calvary Cross and the White Triangle upon the Altar. Thus the station of the Hierophant's Throne fitly represents the rising of the Sun of Life and Light upon our Order (see Figure 2).

The mantle or cloak, plus the robe of scarlet, represents the flaming energy of the Divine Light shining forth through infinite worlds. It is shown in Figure 25. Upon the left breast of the cloak, there is a white cross to represent the purification unto the Light. The white cross on the mantle is a Calvary Cross, which alludes to the Four Rivers of Eden as well as to the suffering to bring about redemption. In the Z.1 document, there is some confusion as to the terms "robe" and "mantle" and their colors. The statement that all members on the Dais wore white robes contradicts earlier statements that robe colors were varied according to the color of the office. In the New Zealand Order, the robes are the same color as the mantle for the officers on the Dais. One version of the Z.1 at Whare Ra, which was reputedly copied from Wynn Westcott's copy, had the reference to the officers of the Dais wearing white robes crossed out, with the note "refer to the above.—S.A." "S.A." was Westcott's Order motto. Taylor was of the opinion that those on the Dais functioned much better through total colors than through partial ones.

Figure 26
The Lamen of the Hierophant

The lamen of the Hierophant, shown in Figure 26, is partially explained in the Portal Ceremony thus:

The Hierophant's Lamen is a synthesis of Tiphareth, to which the Calvary Cross of the six squares, forming the cube opened out, is fitly referred. The two colors, red and green, the most active and the most passive, whose conjunction points out the most practical application of the knowledge of equilibrium, are symbolic of the reconciliation of the celestial essences of Fire and Water. For the reconciling yellow unites with blue in green, which is the complementary color to blue. The small inner circle placed upon the Cross alludes to the Rose that is conjoined therewith in the symbolism of the Rose and Cross of our Order.

But, in addition to this, it represents the blazing light of the Fire of the Sun bringing into being the green vegetation of the otherwise barren Earth and also the power of self-sacrifice requisite in one who would essay to initiation into the sacred Mysteries. The lamen affirms the qualification necessary to him/her who uses it. Therefore, it is suspended from a white collar to represent the purity of the White Brilliance from Kether. Hence, it should always be worn by the Hierophant.

The scepter, shown in Figure 27, represents the Authority and Power of the Light. It is the smallest of the scepters held by those officers on the Dais, being no more than 20 inches in length. It represents the forces of the Middle Pillar. It is scarlet in color, with three gold bands on the shaft. These represent the Sephiroth of Daath, Tiphareth, and Yesod. The gold pommel at the base represents Malkuth. The shaft itself represents the Paths of Gimel, Samekh, and Tau. The grip, by which it is wielded, is the Path of Tau (the lowest portion of the shaft), representing the Universe governed by and attracting the forces of the Light.

The Names of the Sephiroth and Paths are not marked thereon, but the Hierophant Initiate of the Second Order should remember the sublimity of the symbolism while s/he wields it. It represents touching the Divine Light of Kether and attracting it through the Middle Path to Malkuth. It is called the "Scepter of Power" and invests him/her with the power of declaring the Temple Open or Closed in any Grade of the Outer Order. If time is short, then this is done by saying, "By the Power in me vested by

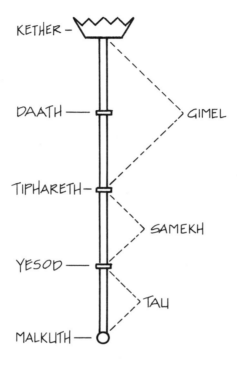

Figure 27
The Scepter of the Hierophant

this Scepter, I declare this Temple duly Opened (or Closed)." This method of Opening and Closing by Scepter should be only used in great emergencies, when time is pressed. It should not be used in a Ceremony where Elemental Spirits have been invoked.

The use of the scepter during ritual is not merely a vacant gesture of pointing it at the desired object for an effect. The scepter becomes an extension of the link between the Hierophant and the Second Order. It represents the power of Osiris, even when s/he takes the form of Aroueris. Once s/he has assumed the Astral Shell of Osiris, s/he then invokes this power to act through the scepter. It becomes a living extension and fusion of Osiris. When the scepter is pointed or directed during the 0=0 ceremony, the power is directed through the Sephirah of Malkuth (at the base of the shaft); this then rises through the shaft, emitting the 12 rays through the miter-headed top of 12 points. These are in the color of the Queen Scale of Briah which, when united, form a White Brilliant Light.

In some Temples, this scepter had a crown of ten points, each representing a Sephirah. However, the rays they emitted were not considered balanced enough, and, though powerful, it was found by clairvoyant members that they were somewhat erratic. It sometimes took a great deal of effort for the Hierophant to control them. By using a 12-pointed miter, a definite change was felt, and the power of the scepter was definitely increased to a higher and more directionable level.

J. W. Brodie-Innes wrote a letter to Felkin about the imbalance of the ten-pointed scepter in 1896, though no solution was offered. Taylor and others at Whare Ra made similar comments. After a great deal of experimentation by Thoth-Hermes members, a 12-pointed miter head was found to be ideal.

The method by which the Hierophant utilizes this force is through his/her Tiphareth center. To be able to do this correctly, his/her sphere of sensation (aura) must be united (the joining of the Ruach and Neshamah) before the start of the ritual, through the scepter (used to call down the power) from the Second Order. As stated above, it must not be wielded for the invocation of Elemental Spirits. Its main function is to prepare a way through for the Light. Its action is literally based on a magnetic charge (hence the magnetized rod up through its shaft—like the Elemental Wand of the Adepti) to blast a path. Using this for Elemental invocations would be disastrous, as the ceremonies form an entirely different function to an Invocation through the Pentagram Ritual.

To give an example, the misuse of a scepter would be to use it to perform Regardie's brilliant "Opening by Watchtower" ceremony (which was based on the Consecration Ceremony of the Vault of the Adepti). In this instance, one would have a First Order Weapon being used through a Second Order Framework of Elemental Invocations, through the Invoking Ritual of the

Pentagram—the very thing the original Z.1 warns against (the correct weapons to use during the Opening by Watchtower are the Elemental Weapons or the Second Order Wand of the Chief Adepti).

The result of this ceremony would be that the power of the scepter would do little but inflate or falsify the Ego, having little or no effect on the actual result. A clairvoyant description of this would be to have red rays of energy emitting from the scepter —directly from the Chief's own auric charge—and not from the Divine Light. This scepter, through repeated use, would be as disastrous (for the wielder) as playing with an atomic pile without protection—with a direct effect on the health of the wielder.

When viewing the correct use of the scepter by clairvoyance, one can see the colored rays form into a white light. Order clairvoyants such as Jack Taylor often informed us that the power of the ceremony can be judged by the effect generated through the use of the scepter. When colors such as red occur, it is because the wielder's magnetic emanations are not coming through the Second Order. (This is not to be confused with the red ray of Tiphareth which is sometimes emitted from this center, but this ray also undergoes a change in color when worked through the Scepter.)

The Banner of the East, shown in Figure 28, is partly explained in the Portal Ritual:

> The field of the Banner of the East is White, the color of light and purity. As in the previous case, the Calvary Cross of six squares is the number six of Tiphareth, the yellow Cross of Solar Gold, and the cubical stone bearing in its center the sacred Tau of Life, and having bound together upon it the form of the Macrocosmic Hexagram, the red triangle of Fire and the blue triangle of Water—the Ruach Elohim and the Waters of Creation.

In addition to this explanation, it affirms the Mode of Action employed by the Divine Light in its operation by the Forces of Nature. Upon it is the symbol of the Macrocosm. This is colored to affirm the action of the Fire of the Spirit through the Waters of Creation under the harmony of the Gold Cross of the reconciler. Within the center of the Hexagram is a Cross in White to represent its action as a Triad. The whole is placed on a white field representing the ocean of the Ain Soph Aur.

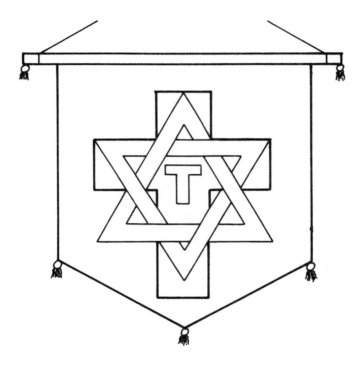

Figure 28
The Banner of the East

The banner is suspended from a gold-colored bar by red cords. The pole and base should be white. The base represents the purity of the foundation—the shaft, the Purified Will directed to the Higher. The golden cross-bar is that whereon the manifested Law of Perfection rests; the banner itself represents the perfect Law of the Universe, the red cords and tassels the divine self-renunciation, the trials and sufferings of which form, as it

were, the Ornament of the Completed Work. The whole represents the ascent of the initiate into Perfect Knowledge of the
Light. Therefore, in the address of the Hiereus, the Neophyte
hears, "Even the Banner of the East sinks in Adoration before
Him," as though that symbol, great and potent though it be, were
yet but an inferior presentiment of the Higher fitted to our
comprehension.

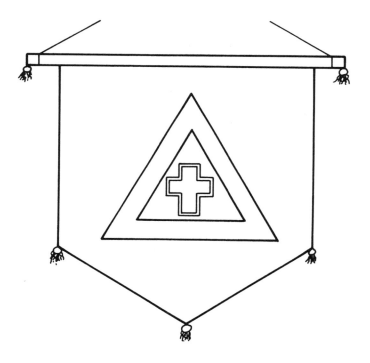

Figure 29
The Banner of the West

In simple terms, the Banner of the East helps fuse the link of
the Hierophant to the Candidate. It also helps prevent obstruc-
tion to this link by its use as a shield that is designed to cast out
the negative aspects before it by absorbing them into it. Since
only the perfected work can be absorbed, the negative influences

are left aside. Again, this is not done through the mere action of holding the banner in front of one, but is done through the use of the Ruach of the Hierophant who activates it (by AHIH) to bring the light through and blind the negative forces. It helps the Candidate go deeper into his or her self and get more benefit out of the ceremony. As a mere symbol, though, it still has quite an effect and helps counterbalance the Banner of the West, which is shown in Figure 29.

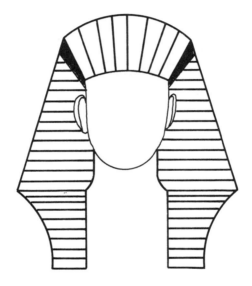

Figure 30
The Nemyss of the Hierophant (front view)

The red-and-white-striped nemyss worn by the Hierophant is colored in a mixture of the Divine Flame through the Divine White Brilliance, both an equal mixture (see Figures 30, 31, and 32). This covers the head of the Hierophant and the Kabbalistic Supernals (the three Sephiroth of Kether, Chokmah, and Binah) in man the Microcosm. The nemyss becomes the Hierophant's link with his/her Ruach to the Astral Shell of Horus and Aroueris that s/he has created. The covering of the Three Higher Sephiroth of Kether, Chokmah, and Binah prevents this acti-vated shell from taking over totally the personality of the

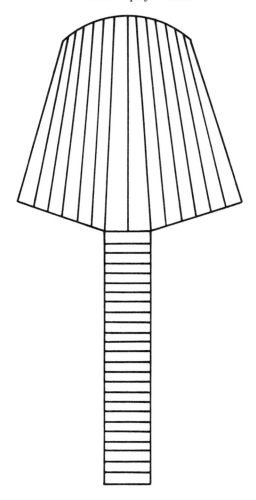

Figure 31
The Nemyss of the Hierophant (rear view)

Hierophant during god-form linkage, yet it does so without repelling it. Normally, this influx of energy would boost up the etheric centers to the point that the Hierophant's own chakras, on his/her back, would be linked directly to those of the god-form, but the nemyss prevents this. The long tail of the nemyss, which goes to just below the base of the spine and is wide enough to cover the chakra vortex, also acts as a type of protection against

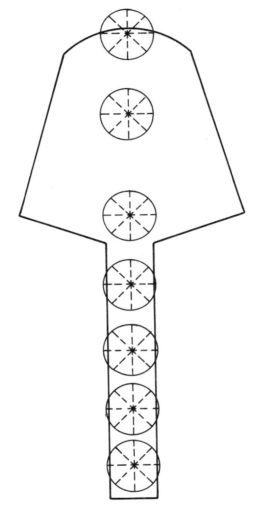

Figure 32
The Sephiroth on the Nemyss of the Hierophant

possession during the ceremony and prevents the kundalini from rising up this path.

Some Adepti, of both the Golden Dawn and the Stella Matutina, had a fear of possession so strong that they had talismans sown into the linings of their nemysses, at the bases of the tails, to prevent this. Though the Golden Dawn recognized the Western Tradition, its members were still very much aware of the effect of the chakras. Felkin's notes show that this type of teaching was taught as early as 1897 to Golden Dawn Adepti.

When the god-forms link to the Hierophant, it is done at the front of the body and not the back, through the lamen, which also acts against possession through the Rose Cross symbols and has control over the Hierophant faculties. At Whare Ra the Hierophant's lamen was sometimes colored white instead of green, which, according to Taylor, helped keep the link to the astral god-form pure and prevented obsession better than green though still retaining its function while making the link and the god-form more powerful. The use of white or green on the lamen depended entirely on the Hierophant, and both were used for many years.

The Hierophant and the Current of Osiris

The Osirian Current in the Neophyte Ritual is represented in the Outer Order by the Hierophant. It is essentially a current of death and rebirth. The Osirian influence was one of the first major cultures to elevate man to god status. He was the ruler of all eternity. In ancient Egypt, Osiris's main center of worship was in Abydos (Upper Egypt).

Osiris was "Lord of Abydos" and "Lord of Tuat." The latter title refers to that place of limbo to which the dead go before they are judged. The description of this is shown in *The Book of the Dead,* in the "Coming Forth by Day" chapters. From this, it can be seen that the current of Osiris is initiatory. The various stops and lessons given by the Hierophant are the Golden Dawn version of the "Coming Forth by Day" chapters.

Within the ancient Heliopolitan system, Osiris was placed in a subordinate position to Ra, the Sun God. However, in the 0=0 ceremony, he is analogous to Ra, in much the same way as Christ was subordinate to his Father in Heaven. The Osirian influence, in the 0=0 ceremony, is like the "Book of Pylons" which was considered by Budge as a companion to the "Coming Forth by Day" chapters of *The Book of the Dead.*

The Osirian Current is used to establish a Portal or mini-universe within the 0=0 ceremony. It is used to show the Higher Self, through a virtual mass attack on the psyche, during this ritual. Furthermore, it shows the "Way" or correct Path which should be taken. The Osirian Current also shows the reverence of magical secrets.

The solar influence of Osiris is one which is imitated in the circumambulation of the Candidate around the Altar. Here, it acts out the passage of the sun as seen from the Earth. The Higher Self of the Candidate unconsciously identifies with this and it solidifies the *kavanah* (intention) of the Candidate. The Divine Light of this circumambulation focuses the Candidate's energy of the Higher Self, in the macrocosmic sense, of the Solar System. The Higher Self then activates a similar current within the body of the Candidate. This phase of the Osirian Current is a form of realization of this current's existence within the Self, which then tries to imitate it. Also, the Osirian influence allows the Candidate to "wash himself clean," which, in Golden Dawn terms, relates to the consecration of the Candidate.

According to tradition, the body of Osiris was cut into 16 pieces. Each of his 16 parts relates to the Golden Dawn system of the 16 elemental sub-divisions. These become parts of the body of the Candidate which are later purified in the four elemental grade rituals (after the 0=0).

Within the Neophyte Ceremony, we are given a glimpse of what will happen in the "Partaking of the Eucharist" when the four Elements on the altar (rose, light, wine, and bread and salt) are felt through the physical senses of the Candidate to give him or her a sense of unity.

The Osirian Current affects the Ruach of the Candidate during the 0=0. Though it does not, at this point, precipitate the linking with the Nephesch, it does bring about an awakening through one's individual unconscious desire—the impetus for linking with the Ruach that is brought about in the 5=6 ritual. The stimulation of the Osirian Current affects the Candidate through the faculties of the Ruach: memory, will, imagination, desire, and reason. All of these parts of the self are stimulated equally. This is the "balancing process of the 0=0," so often described by Golden

Dawn Adepti.

Praemonstrator

The Praemonstrator is the most senior officer on the Dais and represents Chesed and the Grade of 7=4. The actual word "praemonstrator" is from the Latin *praemonstratrare,* "to show forth." This Chief teaches the members of the Outer Order, either personally or through appointed senior members. The office of the Praemonstrator may be identified by the following:

(1) Throne
(2) Mantle
(3) Lamen
(4) Scepter
(5) Nemyss

The blue throne of the Praemonstrator is situated on the Path of Kaph. This Path passes through the Veil on the side of the Pillar of Mercy and, as such, relates to the title of "Intelligence of Conciliation." It is here that the passive energies must be balanced by the Praemonstrator; otherwise the receptivity would absorb too much of this type of energy. The power of Chesed must be formulated and directed by the Praemonstrator, who represents its influence below the Veil. The exaltation of consciousness that this energy represents is here given form. The throne is said to both absorb and conciliate into a governable mass or form.

The proper mantle of office of the Praemonstrator is the Bright Blue Robe of Water, representing the reflection of wisdom and knowledge of Chesed. The White Cross and Triangle represent the purification of the Outer Order by Water. The cross on the mantle of the Praemonstrator is actually a Pyramidal Cross, which is the cross of the elements representing the descent of the divine and angelic forces into the pyramid symbol (this sits above the triangle, representing the symbol of the Golden Dawn). This action relates to the Higher Forces working through an Elemental Symbolism. Beneath this cloth, the Praemonstrator wears a blue robe. The robe is shown in Figure 33.

The Praemonstrator may wear a lamen like that of the

Hierophant, but it is blue upon an orange field and it hangs from a blue collar. The link which the Praemonstrator forms to the god-form Isis is done through his Tiphareth center. The Rose Cross symbol tapers the power so that the link is formed through certain conditions. Its color attracts Isis, and the complimentary orange creates the flashing effect that will make the link on two distinct levels.

Figure 33
The Robe of the Praemonstrator

The scepter of the Praemonstrator has a blue shaft with a single gold band one quarter of the way up the shaft and one at its base (see Figure 34). Upon this is mounted a Maltese Cross in the colors of the Elemental Tablets, from North going clockwise: Yellow, Blue, Black, and Red. The first yellow band, on the base of the scepter, represents Malkuth. The next, Netzach, and the shaft above Netzach is Kaph. The rest of the shaft represents Qoph. The grip is on the Path of Kaph, which shows the influence

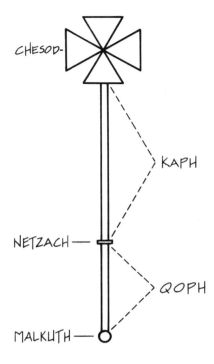

Figure 34
The Scepter of the Praemonstrator

above the Veil and represents the power of the "Wheel" and the cyclic nature of its existence. Since the power of this Office is above Malkuth, the lower grip is never used lest it interfere with the actions of the Hierophant. The Pyramidal Cross mounted on top of the scepter shows the elements consolidating the Water influence (with Earth, the densest element touching the shaft) so that it can be controlled and directed.

Since the Hierophant's Scepter works through Malkuth, the Praemonstrator's works through Netzach (from Kaph). The Scepter's use is mainly for receiving power from the Veil and to activate the Praemonstrator's Sphere of Chesed on the Dais. It also activates that of Netzach, which is the Pillar of Mercy on the Temple Floor, and keeps the power flowing through so that the temple is properly balanced.

(5) The nemyss of the Praemonstrator is Blue with complementary orange stripes. The function of this is the same as the Hierophant's nemyss, save that the colors represent the blue of water balanced with its flashing color from the astral plane.

The Praemonstrator and the Current of Isis

The Current of Isis is activated by the Praemonstrator. On the floor of the Temple, her influence is in the shape of the Pillar of Mercy, in the station of Netzach. Isis was the epitome of motherhood to the ancient Egyptians. She was the sister/wife of Osiris. She used her magical formula to give life to her dead husband. Her function was to prepare the way for her deceased husband through prayer. Apart from her general functions, Isis's specialty was vibration. It was she who said the words to rescue Osiris and bring him back to life. Isis represents Wisdom and Knowledge, which are given out in the speeches of the Temple officers during the 0=0 ceremony.

Within the Neophyte ceremony, the energies of Isis are Jupiterian by nature. She instills in the Candidate the cause of his own ignorance of the Sacred Mysteries. In this, she gives him direction and motivation. This relates directly to soul growth and provides the attunement to the Candidate's Ruach to blend in with the other energies directed down during the ceremony. Her function is to bind together, with the Candidate, the energy of the group Soul of the Order. She does this by linking the Ruach of the Candidate within the Ruach of the ritual, so that the macrocosmic plan gradually starts to be revealed to him.

The particular faculty she works through, in the Candidate, is memory—the most binding factor associated to the Ruach. She imprints on the unconscious mind of the Candidate the key points of the ceremony that will prepare him for the next level. The Isis Current allows the Candidate's Ruach to have access to the occult symbology of the Universal Unconscious, for Isis makes the Candidate "feel" part of the Order. It is her duty to link together all of the basic 0=0 ceremonies into a cohesive labyrinth that adds to the foundation of the basic Order itself.

The Isis Current acts to make the individual lose the quality of

the "I" for the "we" to participate in the overall plan. She is also
the instigator to unleash the Candidate's "creative abilities"
within the Order framework.

The Egyptian *Book of the Dead* says of Isis: "O Isis, Thou
Goddess, Thou glorious one, who hast knowledge how to use Thy
mouth." This specifically relates to the intent and aspirations of
the invocation. She must supply each of the officers on the
Temple floor with enough of this type of energy to reach deep
within themselves so that they can give true statements; i.e.,
statements which are both meant and felt, and not merely read
as empty words. In other terms, she helps the officers achieve the
correct vibrational pitch so that all may act in unison and with
fervor when speaking during the ceremony. When word fumbles
occur during speeches in this ritual, then the Isis Current is not
manifesting correctly.

The Isis energy also assists with the consecration of both the
Temple and the Candidate. She re-enforces the Current of Osiris
in that function. Also, it is she who instills the solemnity of the
occasion when the Candidate is stopped and questioned during
the ritual. It is also through her efforts that the Candidate is
allowed to pass on to the next point.

Within the Golden Dawn, Stella Matutina, and Smaragdum
Thalasses, the words "dead air" are used to refer to a ritual when
nothing seemed to happen. This relates directly back to the
duties of the Praemonstrator whose function it is to activate and
outwardly direct the Current of Isis during ritual. When this
Officer is not performing his function correctly, "dead air" creeps
into the ritual. To direct and use the Isis Current requires a great
deal of work from the Praemonstrator, for he or she must
reinforce the Hierophant at all times (through the Ruach).

Imperator

The Imperator is the Chief who holds the IMPERIUM, the
rule, command, or charge over the Outer Order. It is s/he who is
in charge of the Temple. S/he conducts the ceremonies and is
responsible for the general discipline of the Order. The Imperator
relates to the Sephira of Geburah, the god-form of Horus, and the

rank of 6=5 within the Order. This officer may be identified by the following:

(1) Throne
(2) Mantle, robe
(3) Lamen
(4) Sword
(5) Nemyss

The red throne of the Imperator sits on the Path of Mem, has the title of "Stable Intelligence," and relates to growth through a given framework. His or her position is at the far left of the Temple. As such, it represents the Pillar of Severity, which directly relates to the martial qualities of masculine force. It is here that one comes through the suffering of Spiritual Initiation—the first step on the path to illumination. This path is the opposite of Kaph, as here one is virtually on trial—while in Kaph one transcended this state. The Imperator's Throne is the place where one's competence is tested.

The mantle of the Imperator is a flame-scarlet robe—the cloak of Fire and Severity. The energy and stability of the Temple depend on the Imperator (see Figure 35). The cloak and robe are the symbols of unflinching Authority, compelling the obedience of the Temple to all commands issued by the Second Order. Upon the left breast of the robe is the Maltese Cross above a triangle. The Maltese Cross of four arrowheads represents the keen and swift impact of the Light coming from behind the Veil.

The lamen of the Imperator is similar to that of the Hierophant (and performs the same functions) save it is hung from a green collar. This shows that s/he takes a commanding, but passive, role compared to that of the Hierophant.

The sword of the Imperator has a red grip with a gold guard (see Figure 36). The grip represents the Path of Shin, while the gold is Tiphareth, and the blade is Mem with Geburah as the tip. Wielding from the power of Shin shows the power of "Perpetual Intelligence," for this is a weapon used blade-on only. The Imperator sits with the sword partly turned so the edge of the blade faces towards the Temple. It acts as a warning to any

Figure 35
The Robe of the Imperator

elemental or higher force that this is the Sword of Judgment that will inflict retribution on anything that interferes with the ceremony.

The nemyss is red with green stripes and has a similar function to that of the Hierophant.

The Imperator and the Current of Nepthys (or Nephthys)

On the Dais, the goddess Nepthys is represented by the Imperator and, on the Temple floor, by the Black Pillar in the Station of Hod. In Egyptian mythology, Nepthys was the sister to both Isis and Osiris and was considered by many as the shadow of Isis, always in the background—ready to be counted on if needed. It was Nepthys who helped Isis reconstruct the body of Osiris. It was she who was instrumental in helping Horus after he was stung by the scorpion. Her main centers of worship were at Senu, Hebet, Per-mert, and Re-nefert. Her functions are described in

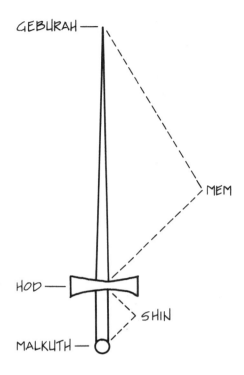

Figure 36
The Sword of the Imperator

The Book of the Dead, where she says, "I go round behind Osiris. I have come that I may protect Thee, and my strength which protecteth shall be behind Thee forever." Nephthys was considered the extremity of things—which referred namely to boundaries. She was also associated with death and rebirth.

The function of Nephthys in the 0=0 ceremony is to stabilize the currents from North to South and East to West. As such, it has an influence on the Altar, the point where all these meet. She also has control of the Canopic Gods (or Four Children of Horus, as they are sometimes called) situated at each corner of the temple. With the Imperator as the tool, Nephthys's current is one of power, in working at the Altar, in which she assists the Osirian Current. While initiating a current in the Temple is one thing, maintaining it is yet another. To balance these currents in an even flow is the responsibility of the Imperator and the Current of Nepthys.

During the 0=0 ceremony, when the Higher Self of the Neophyte is placed between the Pillars, it is the function of the Nepthys Current to hold it, or bind it to this position, so that it does not wander off during the ritual. If Nepthys were to relax her vigilance, Typhon would then try to seize the Ruach of the Neophyte. Every position of every god-form owes its stability to the Current of Nepthys. If she were not present, the Portal, or boundary of the ritual, would be opened. One of the major functions of Nepthys is to contain the limits of the Portal during the ceremony. She accomplishes this through the Imperator. She binds the god-forms so they remain in their correct stations through the power emanating from the Altar and the Osirian Current.

When the god-forms move around the Temple floor, Nepthys has to maintain the correct balance of energy which she works through the Pillars. It is Nepthys who holds and conceals the Ruach of the Neophyte from Typhon in the place of Harpocrates. When Typhon tries to move out, Nepthys assists Horus/Aroueris to keep him at bay. When the Neophyte enters the Temple, it is Nepthys who keeps him from straying from the allotted path during the ritual. In the final part of the ceremony, when members partake in the Eucharist to help ground the varying energies into their auras, the Nepthys Current is responsible for seeing that no negative energies are taken in with the good.

It is the duty of the Nepthys Current to prevent any negative influence on the ability of the Imperator to create and assume a god-form. If this is not done properly, the Portal remains weak and can be penetrated. At the conclusion of the ceremony, it is she who must dissolve the Portal and any forms in it and ensure that no trace of residue remains.

Cancellarius

The Cancellarius is the officer who represents the Sphere of Tiphareth. The actual etymology of the word *cancellarius* is derived from the (late) Latin word meaning "porter," "door-keeper," or "secretary." It is the origin of the English word "chancellor," originally an usher in a law court, then a keeper of the records, a secretary (in which sense it is used in Shakespeare). In later years, this word referred specifically to the king's secretary, the officer to whom petitions for the mitigation of the rigor of the common law were referred. He became the "Keeper of the King's Conscience" and acquired judicial functions which developed into the Court of Chancery. Until about the end of the 16th century, he was an ecclesiastic; afterwards, a lawyer.

The generally accepted derivation of his name is from the position of his seat near the *cancelli* or lattice-work partition surrounding the Judgment Seat. Others have suggested that it is derived (like the word "cancel") from crossing out words with a lattice-like line. The Roman numeral X, for "ten," originated in the practice of crossing every tenth stroke, the upper half of the X being taken to represent half of this, the Roman V, which stands for "five."

In the Order, the Cancellarius is the Secretary of the Temple who keeps the Roll of Membership, who is in charge of and issues the manuscripts, and who keeps a record of the progress of every member. In the event of resignation or expulsion of a member, the Cancellarius cancels his name in the official records of the Temple. He is more immediately than either of the proceeding Chiefs the Representative of the executive authority of the Second Order over the Outer. The Cancellarius is identified by the following:

(1) Throne
(2) Mantle and robe
(3) Lamen
(4) Scepter
(5) Nemyss

The yellow-gold throne of the Cancellarius represents the Sephirah of Tiphareth and sits on the Path of Samekh, which leads to Yesod, the Sephiroth of Air.

The mantle and robe of the Cancellarius are colored in the yellow gold of Air and the Sephirah of Tiphareth (see Figure 37).

Figure 37
The Robe of the Cancellarius

The White Cross (situated above the triangle) on the mantle is an equilateral one which represents the Cross of the Elements and symbolizes their purification through the Light of the four-lettered name, YHVH, in Tiphareth. The Cross above the Triangle relates to the purification of the Outer Order by Air.

The Cancellarius wears a lamen like that of the Hierophant, but of yellow on a purple field and hanging from a purple collar. The function of this is exactly the same as the lamen of the other officers on the Dais.

The scepter of the Cancellarius is surmounted by a hexagram of amber and gold (see Figure 38). The hexagram relates to Tiphareth, the main shaft of the scepter to Samekh, the white ring above the grip to Yesod, the grip to Resh, and the pommel to Malkuth. By working through the path of Resh, through Yesod, the Cancellarius is able to use the solar energy by bringing through the Divine Light of Thoth the Enterer, without whom no

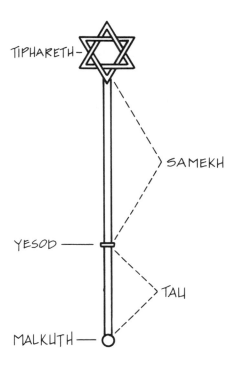

Figure 38
The Scepter of the Cancellarius

connection to the Second Order can be made.

(5) The nemyss is gold with mauve or purple stripes and has the same function as that of other nemysses.

The Cancellarius and the Current of Thoth

The god-form of Thoth is represented by the Cancellarius on the Dais. Thoth was always considered the Scribe of the Gods. It was on his records that the fate of the deceased depended. Thoth was self-created. He taught the sciences and gave the world divine speech. It is said that his name was derived from the word "weight." In ancient Egypt, his main center of worship was in Khemennu.

Within the 0=0 ritual, Thoth holds a very unique position, for he is the personal representative of the Second Order. It is he that makes sure that the Current of Thoth (from the Second Order) is given to the right person. Also, it is he who makes judgment if this current is to be instilled in the Candidate. All the invocations in the world will not work unless the god-form of Thoth is formulated correctly by the Cancellarius so that the powers may find the correct resting place. It is he who must judge the past performance of the Candidate before admittance to the Order.

If the Candidate is considered unsuitable by this god-form, then the energy impregnated into his aura is merely nothing but residue of the ritual's other currents. If the individual going through the 0=0 is found unsuitable by Thoth, then any future gestures will only produce some psychological effect (this includes Inner Order positions as well). Thoth is representative of the Inner Order, while the Hierophant merely acts on their behalf. Thoth must be correctly formulated and his energies directed at the Candidate by the actions of the Ruach of the Cancellarius, for without this the ritual cannot function.

Past Hierophant

The duties of the Past Hierophant, or Previous Hierophant, in the 0=0 ceremony is mainly one of a support role. S/he wears the same costume as the Hierophant (in some Temples the Past Hierophant wears a pure scarlet nemyss to distinguish his/her office from that of the Hierophant). S/he usually carries the Hierophant's scepter while the new Hierophant is "learning the ropes." S/he is there to support and train the new Hierophant and, if the former makes an error in judgment, to step in and help. S/he may, from time to time, give some advice to the Hierophant during the ritual as well. When the Hierophant leaves the Dais to work on the Temple floor, the Past Hierophant then assumes the vacant slot and takes over during the Hierophant's absence.

The Past Hierophant and the Current of Aroueris

The god-form of Aroueris in its Golden Dawn context represents Horus the Elder. He was analogous to the "Light of the

Adepts of the Ra Horakhty Temple in ceremonial dress

Beginning of the Sign of the Enterer
(demonstrated by Frater M.L.)

The Sign of the Enterer

The Sign of Silence

Hiereus, Hierophant, and Hegemon:
The Officers of the Middle Pillar

The Hegemon, Hiereus, and Hierophant hold their weapons over the head of the Candidate following her acceptance into the Order.

The Kerux, with lamp, leads the circumambulation past the Banner of the West.

Day," the one who fought Set (as Night). His seat of power in ancient Egypt was at Makenut and Sakhemat. In the 0=0 ritual, he is represented by the station of the Past Hierophant, whose function is to activate this god-form on the Dais when the Hierophant is on the Temple floor.

His or her actual duty on the Temple floor is to protect the Higher Self of the Candidate from being taken over at critical points of the ceremony. S/he faces his old adversary, Typhon, when he tries to leave his station of the Evil One to do damage and cause havoc in the ritual. This type of protective duty that Aroueris performs is also shared slightly with the god-form of Harpocrates, whose Invisible Station prevents the Evil One from taking the power of the Circumambulation. Aroueris is very much the guardian on the floor and protects not only the Candidate but the Officers as well.

While s/he functions on the Temple floor, Aroueris has the duty to control the power or current which the Hierophant has initiated in the East as well. S/he does not actually create this current, but guards it to make sure that it functions correctly. In modern terms, his/her duty on the Dais is like that of a maintenance man; while on the floor, he is a type of shock trooper. While the Current of Aroueris comes from the Hierophant's Throne, Aroueris' astral form gives it an additional boost both in strength and direction. The Past Hierophant must control the power from his/her own station (beside the Hierophant) through his/her Ruach which is linked to the Ruach of the ceremony itself. When the Hierophant uses the power on the Temple floor, it is through the form of Aroueris on the Dais, and the astral form of Aroueris then envelopes him/her.

Because of Aroueris' martial-like position on the Temple floor, his/her position of power in the 0=0 is one of extremes. From one viewpoint, s/he upholds the power of the Hierophant and, in other areas, s/he treads on Typhon, thus containing him. S/he is very much the warring priest combination. The Current of Aroueris is one of sudden transformations and changes. It is one that takes the subtle centers of the Candidate to the limit of his or her abilities (within the 0=0 terms of reference) and it also speeds up the vibration of the Candidate so that s/he can assimilate the data, that is received more rapidly in a complete upheaval by a revolutionary attitude. The Candidate then becomes the focal point for Universal Consciousness of the Order to flow into. If this touch by Aroueris is not reciprocated by the Candidate s/he will simply withdraw it. It is then that s/he implants a radical sense of change in the Candidate through the Ruach.

Hiereus

The Station of the Hiereus is at the extreme West of the Temple and the lowest point of Malkuth, where s/he is enthroned in its darkest part in the quarter represented black in the figure of the Minutum Mundum. Representing a terrible and avenging god at the confines of matter, at the borders of the Qlippoth, s/he is enthroned upon matter and robed in Darkness, and about his/her feet are thunder and lightning—the impact of the Paths of Shin and Qoph, Fire and Water, terminating respectively in the russet and olive quarters of Malkuth. There, therefore, is s/he placed as a mighty and avenging guardian to the Sacred Mysteries. The symbols and insignia of Hiereus are:

(1) The Throne of the West in the black of Malkuth, where it borders on the Kingdom of Shells.

(2) The Black Robe of Darkness, bearing a White Cross on the left breast.

(3) The Sword of Strength and Severity.

(4) The lamen suspended from a scarlet collar.

(5) The Banner of the West.

Note: The nemysses of the officers on the floor are black with white stripes, the exception being the Hegemon, whose nemyss is pure white. These perform the same functions as the nemysses of the Officers on the Dais.

The position of the Throne of the West, at the Limits of Malkuth, is fitting for the Avenger of the Gods, for s/he is placed there in eternal affirmation against the Evil One—"Hitherto shall ye come and no further." The Throne is also placed there as a seat of witness and of punishment decreed against Evil.

Basically, the Throne has two functions: to prevent the Qlippoth from entering and to prevent anyone lingering outside this area from entering through curiosity.

The position of the Throne is the easiest access for any negative traits—for this is the area where the Sun, or Light of Day, sinks into oblivion. The Throne of the Hiereus contains this by keeping the forces of Light (directly from the Hierophant) focused on the locked gateway of the West.

Figure 39
The Robe of the Hiereus

The robe and mantle of the Hiereus symbolize Darkness, threatening and terrible to the Outer, as concealing an avenging force ever ready to break forth against the Evil Ones (see Figure 39). On the left breast is a White Cross to represent the Purification of Matter unto the Light. Taylor always taught that, though the robe and mantle were the same color, they worked on different principles. The mantle or cloak was the active part of

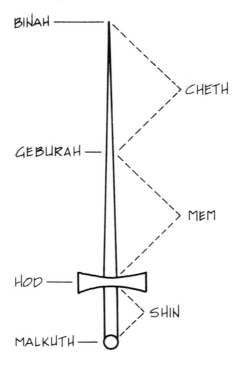

Figure 40
The Sword of the Hiereus

the Hiereus while the robe, like those of all the officers on the
Temple floor (save Hegemon), was black because of its absorption
principle. The black restricts the growth of negativity, which
bogs it down by condensing it. Before any negativity can work on
the Temple Officers, it must try to take over the god-form the
officer represents, and the black robe prevents this by absorbing
all its energy and restricting it—which is usually held in check by
the god-form above it. Though not an Earth Grade, the robes of
the Temple Officers draw from the densest part of Malkuth for
their strength. Taylor likened the principle to being caught in a
bog with no escape for any negative force that did not manage to
penetrate the Portal of the Temple. There are of course checks
and counterchecks with the various other energies, so that there
are overlapping safety factors should one or more forces fail to

uphold their function of protection during the ritual.

The sword represents the forces of the Pillar of Severity as a whole (see Figure 40). The guard represents Hod and is usually made of brass; the grip is the Path of Shin which represents the Universe governed by the flaming forces of Severity and which represents Hiereus as wielding the forces of Divine Severity. "The Sword of Vengeance is its Name." The blade shows this concept from Hod to Binah, encompassing Geburah through the paths of Mem and Cheth.

Figure 41
The Lamen of the Hiereus

The lamen (shown in Figure 41) is particularly explained in the Portal Ceremony:

> The Outer Circle includes the four Sephiroth, Tiphareth, Netzach, Hod, and Yesod, of which the first three mark the angles of the triangle inscribed within, while the connecting Paths Nun, Ayin, and Peh form its sides. In the extreme center is the Path Samekh through which is the passage for the Rending of the Veil. It is therefore a fitting Lamen for Hiereus as representing the connecting link between the First and Second Orders, while the white triangle established in the surrounding Darkness is circumscribed in its turn by the Circle of Light.

In addition to this explanation, the lamen represents "The Light that shineth in Darkness though the darkness comprehendeth it not." It affirms the possible Redemption from Evil, and even that of Evil itself, through self-sacrifices. It is suspended from a scarlet collar as representing its dependence on the Forces of Divine Severity, over-awing the evil. It is a symbol of tremendous Strength and Fortitude, and it is a synthesis of the Office of the Hiereus, as regards the Temple, as opposed to his Office as regards the Outer World. For these reasons, it should always be worn by the Hiereus.

The Banner of the West (see Figure 29, page 84) completes the symbols of Hiereus. It is thus explained in the Zelator Grade:

> The White Triangle refers to the three Paths connecting Malkuth with the other Sephiroth; while the red cross is the Hidden Knowledge of the Divine Nature which is to be obtained through their aid. The Cross and Triangle together represent Life and Light.

In addition to this explanation from the Zelator Grade, it represents eternally the possibility of Rescuing the Evil; but, in it, the Tiphareth cross is placed within the White Triangle of the Supernals as thereby representing the sacrifice as made only unto the Higher. The Red Cross may be bordered with gold, in this instance, to represent the perfect metal obtained in and through the Darkness of Putrefaction. Black is its field, which thus represents the Darkness and Ignorance of the Outer, while the White Triangle is again the Light which shineth in the Darkness but which is not understood. Therefore is the Banner of the West the symbol of Twilight—as it were the equation of Light and Darkness. The pole and base are black, to represent that even in the depths of Evil can that symbol stand. The cord is black, but the transverse bar and lance-point may be golden or brass and the tassels scarlet, as in the case of the Banner of the East and for the same reasons.

The Banner of the West, when it changes its position in the Temple, represents that which bars and threatens and demands (a symbolic) fresh sacrifice so that the path leading to the Higher can be attained. "Avenger of the Gods" is the name of Hiereus, and s/he is "Horus in the Abode of Blindness unto, and ignorance of, the Higher." Hoor is his name.

Hegemon

The Hegemon is one of the three Chief Officers of the Temple. S/he comes without the Portal and instructs the Candidate to hold him/herself in readiness for the Ceremony of Admission—and also superintends his/her preparation for this by the Sentinel. The name of this Officer is simply a translation from the Greek which means "a leader" or "guide"—"one who has authority over others," and "one who shows the way', "a person who does something first"—"a Commander." It is also found with feminine adjectives from very early times. If we take the verb *ago* from the root AG it means "to carry," "to convey," and "to bring" (mostly with living creatures and objects), "to take with one," "to lead." Also this word relates to "train" or "educate" and to "weigh in a balance." In its adjectival form, *ho hegemononios* has a meaning of guiding and was an epithet of Hermes as the Guide of the Departed Souls (in which capacity this God was known as *Pompaios* or *Psychopompos*). As one can see, its etymological base is highly complex—the guiding of living creatures towards a desired object, at the same time training and weighing it in the balance.

The Station of the Hegemon is between the two Pillars whose bases are in Nezach and Hod, at the intersection of the Paths of Peh and Samekh in the symbolic gateway of Occult Sciences—as it were, at the Base of Balance, at the Equilibrium of the Scales of Justice, at the point of intersection of the lowest reciprocal Path with that of Samekh, which forms part of the Middle Pillar.

This is one position where the feminine, passive energies are usually handled better by a woman than a man. At Whare Ra, this position was usually taken by a woman, and I believe it was the same in the Golden Dawn. S/he is placed there as the Guardian of the Threshold of Entrance and the Preparer of the Way of the Enterer—therefore the reconciler between the Light and Darkness and the mediator between the Stations of the

Hierophant and the Hiereus.

The Hegemon has in fact three Coptic forms: 1. Thma-As-St (as regards the Middle Pillar and the influence from Kether), 2. Thma-aesh (her more Fiery influence related to the Pillar of Severity), and 3. Thmaa-ett (more Fluidic with regard to her influence with respect to the Pillar of Mercy). The symbols and insignia of the Hegemon are:

(1) The robe, nemyss and Mantle of Pure Whiteness, bearing on the left breast a Red Cross.

(2) The miter-headed scepter

(3) The lamen suspended from a black collar.

The robe, nemyss, and mantle represent the color of spiritual purity which is required in the aspirant to the Mysteries and without which qualification none can pass between the Eternal Pillars. It represents the Divine Light which is attracted thereby and brought to the aid·of the Candidate. It symbolizes the self-sacrifice that is offered for another—to aid him in the attainment of the Light. It also signifies the atonement of error, the Preparer of the Pathway unto the Divine. Upon the left breast is a Cross, usually the Calvary Cross, red to represent the energy of the lower Will purified and subjected to that which is Higher—and thus is the Office of Hegemon especially that of the Reconciler.

The miter-headed scepter (see Figure 42) is the distinctive ensign of the Office of Hegemon. On the Tree of Life, it represents the forces of the Pillar of Mercy. It should be of scarlet with gold bands and a pommel. The two bands represent Chesed and Netzach—the shaft being formed by the Paths of Vau, Kaph, and Qoph, the grip with the pommel in Malkuth. The miter is gold with red mountings, and each point terminates in a ball. The miter is charged with a red Calvary Cross of six squares. This miter represents the wisdom of Chokmah as a duplicated aspect of Kether, attracted by the symbol of self-sacrifice. The scepter is wielded by the forces of Flux and Reflux, shown by the grip being referred to the Path of Qoph, and it represents the attraction into the Universe of the Forces of Divine Mercy. The Sephiroth and

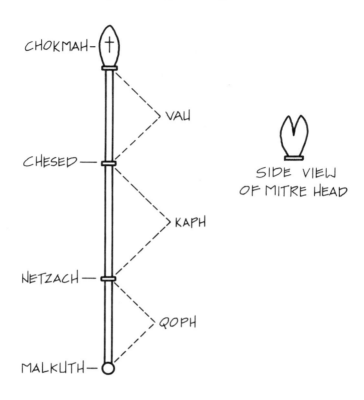

Figure 42
The Scepter of the Hegemon

Paths are marked only as bands and, owing to its meaning,
should be carried by Hegemon in all conducting of the Candidate
as representing to the latter the attraction of the forces of his
Higher Self. It is called the "Scepter of Wisdom." Since the
Hegemon is the wielder of the Scepter of Dual Wisdom from
Chokmah, the miter-head is split in two and not closed, to
indicate the Dual Manifestation of Wisdom and Truth — even as
the Hall of the Neophyte is called "The Hall of the Dual
Manifestation of the Goddess of Truth."

The lamen of the Hegemon (see Figure 43) is explained in part
in the Grade of Philosophus:

Figure 43
The Lamen of the Hegemon

The peculiar emblem of the Hegemon is the Calvary Cross of
Six Squares within a Circle. This Cross embraces Tiphareth,
Netzach, Hod, and Yesod, and rests upon Malkuth. Also the
Calvary Cross of Six Squares forms the cube and is thus
referred to the Six Sephiroth of Microprosopus which are
Chesed, Geburah, Tiphareth, Hod, and Yesod.

In addition to this explanation, it represents the black Calvary
Cross of Suffering, as the Initiator by Trial and Self- Abnegation
and the Opener of the Way into Comprehension of the Forces of
the Divine Light. It is, therefore, suspended from a black collar to
show that suffering is in the Purgation of Evil.

The next three inferior officers do not wear cloaks or mantles,
but only lamens suspended from black collars. The designs are in
white on a black field to show that they are Administrators of the
Forces of Light acting through the darkness, under the Presidency of the Superior Officers.

Kerux

The Kerux is stationed within the Portal of the Hall, and his
duties are to see that the furniture of the Hall is properly
arranged before the opening and to guard the Inner Side of the
Portal. The symbolism of this officer will, as in the case of the
others, gradually unfold itself to the Neophyte as s/he passes

from grade to grade. Also s/he admits the Fratres and Sorores and assists in the reception of the Candidate at the command of the Hierophant, whose Herald or Messenger s/he is. The Greek word *kerux* means "a Herald," "Pursuivant" or "Public messenger," and was equivalent to the Latin word *caduceator* (bearer of the Caducecus), for Hermes was a Herald of the Gods. Their function in ancient Greece was to summon the Assembly (Gr. *ecclesia*), which was originally political and only later became a religious assembly or church) and keep order therein. They had charge of the arrangements at sacrifices and carried wands of office (*skeptron,* from which came "scepter," or *kerukeion,* the latter being usually like the Caduceus). Their persons were sacred and under the protection of Zeus, and they also were messengers between enemies in war. The verb *kerusso* meant "to officiate as a Herald," hence, "to proclaim" (in various senses—e.g., of news of a person's name as a criminal, as winner of a contest, etc.), to summon a person, and then to invoke the Gods or spiritual powers. The Kerux of the Order wears on his/her breast a lamen (from the Latin *lamina,* "a plate" or "thin piece of metal') on which is depicted the Caduceus of Hermes, which relates back to its original Greek meaning. The Kerux is the Herald, the Guardian and Watcher within the temple, as Sentinel is Watcher without—and therefore in his/her charge is the proper disposition of the furniture and stations of the temple. S/he is also the proclaimer. The peculiar ensigns of office are:

(1) Red Lamp
(2) Staff
(3) Lamen

The Red Lamp signifies the Hidden Fire over which s/he watches. The lamp also represents the center of the Ruach, Tiphareth, which the Neophyte aspires to unite with so that the Hidden Knowledge beyond the veil can be revealed.

The Magic Staff of Power (see Figure 44) represents a ray of the Divine Light which kindles the Hidden Fire. In its Outer Order form, this small (un-winged) staff resembles a teacher's pointer and is colored in the three colors (from the top to the point) red,

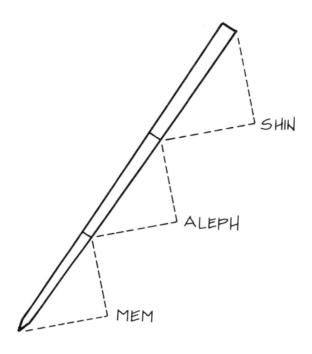

Figure 44
The Staff of the Kerux

yellow, and blue, which represent the three Mother Letters. In its
Inner Order form, this is the Wand of the Chief Adept and is then
shown as a Winged Caduceus, for placed on the Tree of Life the
upper wings touch Chokmah and Binah—the three Supernals.
The seven lower Sephiroth are embraced by the twin serpents
whose heads rest upon Chesed and Geburah. When wielded by
the Kerux, the staff is gripped in the yellow color of Aleph and its
association to Air, which is analogous to the Kerux's nature.

The lamen of the Kerux (see Figure 45) has on it the symbol of
the Winged Caduceus (whose historical significance has been
already explained), whose wings symbolize the transcendence or
rising of the spirit, while the double serpent shows the dualism of
opposites which the Neophyte has to overcome, for the serpent is
the obstacle of man. For it is here in the 0=0 that the Kerux must

Figure 45
The Lamen of the Kerux

guide the Neophyte through the Mystical Circumambulation past the various guards, checks, and balances contained therein.

Stolistes

The Stolistes is the one who equips or clothes, and is a late Greek word equivalent to *hierostolos*—an Egyptian Priest who had charge of the sacred vestments. Neither form of this word is found in the Classical Greek period or in connection with Greek Mysteries. Both belong to the first century A.D. The verb *styello,* and its derivative *stolizo,* mean "to put in train," "to equip," or "dress." *Stolis* signifies "a garment" or "robe," while *stole* (from the same root) means "to equip" or "fit out with clothes" (originally "an army"), hence, "a garment" or "robe." This is the origin of the English word "stole," in the sense of an ecclesiastical vestment (compare with the German word *Bestellen*), though the word *stolisterion* was the vestry of a temple.

The Stolistes is stationed in the northern part of the Hall, to the northwest of the Black Pillar, whose base is in Hod. It is there as an Affirmer of the Powers of Moisture or Water reflected through the Tree into Hod. This office is identified by the following insignia:

Figure 46
The Lamen of Stolistes

(1) Cup
(2) Lamen

The cup is the receptacle filled with the Water from Hod so as to transmit its forces into Malkuth, restoring and purifying the vital forces therein by cold and moisture (see Figure 46). "Goddess of the Scale of the Balance at the Black Pillar" is the name, and she is "The Light Shining through the Waters of the Earth." In the 3=8 grade it says:

> The Cup of Stolistes partakes in part of the Symbolism of the Laver of Moses and the Sea of Solomon. On the Tree of Life, it embraces nine of the Sephiroth, exclusive of Kether. Yesod and Malkuth form the triangle below, the former the apex, the latter the base. Like the Caduceus, it further represents the Three Elements of Water, Air, and Fire. The Crescent is the Water which is above the Firmament, the Circle is the Firmament, and the Triangle the consuming Fire below, which is opposed to the Celestial Fire symbolized by the upper part of the Caduceus.

On the Lamen is the symbol of the cup (see Figure 47).

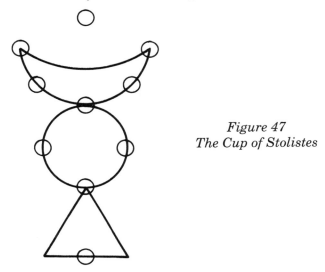

Figure 47
The Cup of Stolistes

Dadouchos

The Dadouchos, meaning, a "torch bearer," was a hereditary officer at the Mysteries of the Eleusinian Demeter, whose torch symbolized her search for her daughter Persephone, the Spirit of Youth and Spring. The verb *daio* means "to kindle," and the word *dadouchos* is compounded of *dais* (or, in Attic Greek, *das*, accusative *dada)*, "a torch," especially a pine torch, and *echo*, "to hold" or "to carry." The Dadouchos, therefore, is posted in the South and symbolizes heat and dryness. S/he attends to the censer and the incense and consecrates the Hall, the members, and the Candidate with Fire. It is an important part of his/her duties to get ready and attend to all lights, fire, and incense used in the ceremonies. The Dadouchos is stationed towards the midst of the southern part of the Hall, to the southwest of the White Pillar whose base is in Netzach, and is there as an Affirmer of the Powers of Fire reflected down the Tree to Netzach. This officer is identified by the following:

(1) The Censer he holds
(2) Lamen

The Censer of the Dadouchos is "the Receptacle of the Powers of Fire" and "the transmitter of the Fire of Netzach to Malkuth," restoring and purifying the vital force therein by heat and dryness. "Goddess of the Scale of the Balance of the White Pillar" is the name of Dadouchos.

Figure 48
The Lamen of Dadouchos

The lamen of the Dadouchos (see Figure 48) is explained in the Zelator grade:

> The Hermetic Cross, which is also called the Fylfot, Hammer of Thor, and Swastika, is formed of 17 Squares taken out of a square of 25 lesser squares. These 17 represent the Sun, the Four Elements, and the Twelve Signs of the Zodiac.

Sentinel

The final officer is the Sentinel, or Phulax, as s/he is sometimes called. His/her name is thought to have been derived from the French, *scentinelle,* or the Italian *sentinella.* Some have even thought that it came from the French *sentier,* "a footpath," which in turn is derived from the Latin, *semita,* "a narrow way." This officer stands in charge of the Candidate at the Portal, or outer opening of the straight and narrow way that s/he is about to enter. The Greek word *phulax* signifies "a Watcher," "guard" or "sentinel"—"guardian" or "keeper." A fuller form of the word is *naophulax,* meaning "keeper of the temple." The verb, *phulasso,* means, "to keep watch and ward," especially by night—and we may think of the Phulax as "the watchman" armed with a lethal weapon to keep out intruders and to prepare the Candidate as s/he stands in the outer darkness.

The Greek word *phulacterion* means "a guarded place," "a fort," or, in its secondary meaning, "a safeguard" or "preservative," "an amulet" for protection, familiar to us from the phylacteries of the Jews, which were strips of parchment inscribed with texts from the Law and worn as amulets on the forehead while praying. The Latin word corresponding to the Greek *phulax* in a general sense is *custos.* The officer is distinguished by the following:

(1) Sword

(2) Lamen

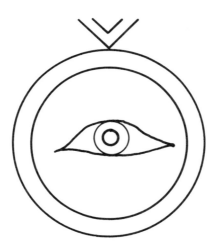

Figure 49
The Lamen of the Sentinel

The Sword of the Sentinel has a black grip and gold guard. The black represents the darkest part of matter, while the gold guard is a reflection of the Hidden Mysteries of the Order. At all times, the sword is drawn and held upright in the left hand (for the duration of the ceremony) as a reminder of the seriousness of the occasion. Even when the Sentinel remains seated beside the door (and outside the Portal, but still inside the Hall), the sword is still drawn.

The symbol of the Eye on the Lamen is that of the Watcher and is quite simplistic compared to some of the Golden Dawn symbolism. The lamen is shown in Figure 49.

The Pillars

From a Paper by Wynn Westcott

In the explanation of the Symbols of the Grade of Neophyte, your attention has been directed to the general mystical meaning of the Two Pillars called in the Ritual the "Pillars of Hermes" of "Seth" and of "Solomon." In the 9th chapter of the Ritual of the Dead they are referred to as the "Pillars of Shu," the "Pillars of the Gods of the Dawning Light," and also as "the North and Southern Columns of the Gate of the Hall of Truth." In the 125th Chapter, they are represented by the sacred gateway, the door to which the aspirant is brought when he has completed the negative confession. The archaic pictures on one Pillar are painted in black upon a white ground, and those on the other in white upon a black ground, in order to express the interchange and reconciliation of opposing forces and the eternal balance of light and darkness which gives force to visible nature.

The black cubical bases represent darkness and matter wherein the Spirit, the *Ruach Elohim,* began to formulate the Ineffable NAME, that Name which the ancient Rabbis have said "rushes through the universe," that Name before which the Darkness rolls back at the birth of time.

The flaming red triangular capitals which crown the summit of the Pillars represent the Triune manifestation of the Spirit of

121

Life, the Three Mothers of the Sepher Yetsirah, the Three Alchemical Principles of Nature, the Sulphur, the Mercury and the Salt.

Each Pillar is surmounted by its own light-bearer veiled from the material world.

At the base of both Pillars rise the Lotus flowers, symbols of regeneration and metempsychosis. The archaic illustrations are taken from vignettes of the 17th and 125th chapters of the Ritual of the Dead, the Egyptian Book of the *Pert-em-Hru* or the *Book of Coming Forth into the Day*, the oldest book in the world as yet discovered [as of Westcott's writing. The Sumerian *Epic of Gilgamesh* is now considered to be much older.—Ed.]. The Recension of the Priests of ON is to be found in the walls of the Pyramids of the Kings of the 5th and 6th Dynasties at Sakarah, the recension of the 11th and 12th Dynasties on the sarcophagi of that period, and the Theban recension of the 18th Dynasty and onward is found on the papyri, both plain and illuminated. No satisfactory translation of these books is available, none having been yet attempted by a scholar having the qualifications of mystic as well as Egyptologist.

The Ritual of the Dead, generally speaking, is a collection of hymns and prayers in the form of a series of ceremonial Rituals to enable the man to unite himself with Osiris the Redeemer. After this union he is no longer called the man, but Osiris, with whom he is now symbolically identified. "That they also may be One of us," said the Christ of the New Testament. "I am Osiris" said the purified and justified man, his soul luminous and washed from sin in the immortal and uncreated light, united to Osiris, and thereby justified, and the son of God; purified by suffering, strengthened by opposition, regenerate through self-sacrifice. Such is the subject of the great Egyptian Ritual.

The 17th Chapter of the Theban recension consists of a very ancient text with several commentaries, also extremely old, and some prayers, none of which come into the scheme of the original text. It has, together with the 12th chapter, been very carefully translated for the purpose of this lecture by the V.H. Frater M.W.T. [Marcus Worsley Blackden], and V.H. Soror S.S.D.D.

[Florence Farr] has made many valuable suggestions with regard to the interpretation. The Title and Preface of the 17th Chapter reads:

> Concerning the exaltation of the Glorified Ones, of Coming and Going forth in the Divine Domain, of the Genies of the Beautiful land of Amentet. Of coming forth in the light of Day in any form desired, of hearing the Forces of Nature by being enshrined as a living Bai.

And the Rubric is:

> The united with Osiris shall recite it when he has entered the Harbour. May glorious things be done thereby upon earth. May all the words of the Adept be fulfilled.

Owing to the complex use of symbols, the ritual translation of the Chapter can only be understood by perpetual reference to the ancient Egyptian commentaries, and therefore the following paraphrase has been put together to convey to modern minds as nearly as possible the ideas conceived by the old Egyptians in this glorious triumphal song of the Soul of Man made one with Osiris, the Redeemer.

> I am Tum made One with all things
>
> I have become NU. I am RA in his rising ruling by right of his Power. I am the Great God self-begotten, even NU, who pronounced His Names, and thus the Circle of the Gods was created.
>
> I am Yesterday and know Tomorrow. I can never more be overcome. I know the secret of Osiris, whose being is perpetually revered of RA. I have finished the work which was planned at the Beginning, I am the Spirit made manifest, and armed with two vast eagle's plumes. Isis and Nephthys are their names, made One with Osiris.
>
> I claim my inheritance. My sins have been uprooted and my passions overcome. I am Pure White. I dwell in Time. I live through Eternity, when Initiates make offering to the Everlasting Gods. I have passed along the Pathway. I know the Northern and the Southern Pillars, the two Columns at the gateway of the Hall of Truth.

Stretch unto me your hands, O ye dwellers in the centre. For I am transformed to a God in your midst. Made One with Osiris, I have filled the eye socket in the day of the morning when Good and Evil fought together.

I have lifted up the cloud-veil in the Sky of the Storm. Till I saw RA born again from out the Great Waters. His strength is my strength, and my strength is His strength. Homage to you, Lords of Truth, chiefs who Osiris rules. Granting release from Sin, followers of Ma where rest is Glorious. Whose Throne Anubis built in the day when Osiris said:

"Lo! A man wins his way to Amentet. I come before you, to drive away my faults. As ye did to the Seven Glorious Ones who follow their Lord Osiris. I am that Spirit of Earth and Sun."

Between the Two Pillars of Flame. I am RA when he fought beneath the Ashad Tree, destroying the enemies of the Ancient of Days. I am the Dweller in the Egg. I am he who turns in the Disc. I shine forth from the Horizon, as the gold from the mine. I float through the Pillars of SHU in the ether. Without a peer among the Gods. The Breath in my mouth is as a flame. I light upon the Earth with my glory. Eye cannot gaze on my darting beams, as they reach through the Heavens and lick up the Nile with tongues of flame. I am strong upon Earth with the Strength of Ra. I have come into Harbour as Osiris made perfect. Let priestly offerings be made to me as one in the train of the Ancient of Days. I brood as the Divine Spirit. I move in the firmness of my Strength. I undulate as the Waves that vibrate through Eternity. Osiris has been claimed with acclamation, and ordained to rule among the gods. Enthroned in the Domain of Horus where the Spirit and the Body are united in the presence of the Ancient of Days. Blotted out are the sins of his body in passion. He has passed the Eternal Gate, and has received the New Year Feast with Incense, at the marriage of Earth with Heaven.

TUM has built his bridal chamber. RURURET has founded his shrine. The procession is completed. HORUS has purified, SET has consecrated, SHU made one with OSIRIS has entered his heritage.

As TUM he has entered the Kingdom to complete union with the Invisible. Thy Bride, O Osiris, is Isis, who mourned Thee when she found Thee slain. In Isis, Thou art born again. From Nephthys is thy nourishment. They cleansed thee in thy Heavenly Birth. Youth waits upon thee, ardour is ready at thy hand. And their arms shall uphold thee for millions of years. Initiates surround Thee and Thine enemies are cast down. The Powers of Darkness are destroyed. The Companions of Thy Joys are with Thee. Thy Victories in the Battle await their reward in the Pillar. The Forces of Nature obey Thee. Thy Power is exceeding great. The Gods curse him that curseth Thee. Thine Aspirations are fulfilled. Thou art the Mistress of Splendour. They are destroyed who barred Thy way.

The 125th Chapter is concerned with the entry of the Initiate into the Hall of the Two Columns of Justice, and commenced with a most beautiful and symbolic description of Death, as a journey from the barren wilderness of Earth, to the Glorious Land which lies beyond. The literal translation of the opening lines is as follows:

> I have come from afar to look upon thy beauties. My hands salute Thy Name of Justice. I have come from afar, where the Acacia Tree grew not. Where the tree thick with leaves is not born. Where there come not beams from herb or grass. I have entered the Place of Mystery. I have communed with Set. Sleep came upon me, I was wrapped therein, bowing down before the hidden things. I was ushered into the House of Osiris. I saw the marvels that were there. The Princes of the Gates in their Glory.

The illustrations in this section represent the Hall of Truth as seen through the open leaves of its door. The Hall is presided over by a God who holds his right hand over the cage of a hawk, and his left hand over the food of eternity. On each side of the God is a cornice crowned by a row of alternate feathers and Uraei symbolizing justice and fiery power. The door leaf which completes the right hand of a stall is called "Possessor of Truth controlling the Feet," while that on the left is "Possessor of strength, binding the male and female animals." The 42 Judges of the Dead are represented as seated in a long row, and each of them has to be named, and the Sin over which he presides has been denied.

This chapter describes the introduction of the initiate into the Hall of Truth by ANUBIS, who, having questioned the aspirant, receives from him an account of his initiation, and is satisfied by his right to enter. He states that he has been taken into the ante-chamber of the Temple and there stripped and blind-folded, he had to grope for the entrance of the Hall, and having found it, he was reclothed and anointed in the presence of the Initiated. He is asked for the Pass-words and demands that his Soul *[ba]* should be weighed in the Great Balance of the Hall of Truth, whereupon ANUBIS again interrogates him concerning the symbolism of the door of the Hall, and his answers being found correct, ANUBIS says: "Pass on, thou knowest it."

Among other things, the Initiate states that he has been puri-fied four times, the same number of times that the Neophyte is purified and consecrated in the ceremony of the Neophyte. He then makes the long Negative Confession, stating to each Judge in turn that he is innocent of that form of Sin over which he judges. Then he invokes the Judges to do him justice, and after-wards describes how he had washed in the washing place of the South, and rested in the North, in the place called "Son of the De-liverers" and he becomes the dweller under the Olive Tree of Peace, and how he was given a tall flame of fire and a sceptre of cloud which he preserved in the salting tank in which mummies were swathed. And he found there another sceptre called "Giver of Breath" and with that he extinguished the flame and shattered the sceptre of cloud, and made a lake of it. The initiate is then brought under the symbol of the Scales of a Balance. He also has to name the Guardian of the Gateway, who prevents his passage, and when all these are propitiated, the plea of the Hall itself cries out against his steps, saying "Because I am silent, because I am pure," and it must know that his aspirations are pure enough and high enough for him to be allowed to tread upon it. He is then al-lowed to announce to Thoth that he is clean from all evil, and has overcome the influence of the planets, and THOTH says to him: "Who is He whose Pylons are of Flame, whose walls of Living Uraei, and the flames of whose House are streams of Water?" And the initiate replies "Osiris"

And it is immediately proclaimed: "Thy meat shall be from the Infinite, and thy drink from the Infinite. Thou art able to go forth to the sepulchral feasts on earth, for thou hast overcome."

Thus, these two chapters which are represented by their illustrations upon the Pillars, represent the advance and purification of the Soul and its union with Osiris, the Redeemer, in the Golden Dawn of the Infinite Light, in which the Soul is transfigured, knows all, and can do all, for it is made One with the Eternal God.

KHABS AM PEKHT

KONX OM PAX

LIGHT IN EXTENSION

The Z.1 document states, "Upon them [the Pillars] should be represented in counterchanged colour *any* appropriate Egyptian designs, emblematic of the Soul." [italics mine]. The bottom line was that most temples had their own Egyptian designs on the Pillars. In many ways, these were similar to the Vaults of various temples who chose their own version of the color schemes but still retained the basic design.

There has been a misconception that the Pillar drawings published by Robert Wang in *The Secret Temple* and also by Regardie in *The Complete Golden Dawn System of Magic* were the *only* ones utilized by the Golden Dawn. The object of the Pillar drawings was to show the procession of the soul in the afterlife and yet try to relate them to the journey of the Candidate in the 0=0 ritual. What has never been discussed in print is that only the White Pillar relates to the 0=0 ritual. The Black Pillar relates to the Inner Order and, as such, only the White Pillar will be discussed here. The Black Pillar will be elaborated on in a separate volume.[1]

The designs shown in Figures 50 through 53 are taken from the two Pillars of the New Zealand Thoth-Hermes Temple. They are

---

[1]The designs for the White Pillar were commonly accepted as for the 0=0. It appears that, when Mathers wrote the Portal Ritual, he had a change of heart and equated the White and Black Pillars with the Order sashes. At Whare Ra, they solved the problem by placing the drawing of Ani entering the Hall of Maat on the Black Pillar—a reversal of what some have written, such as J. W. Brodie-Innes. I have presented it the Brodie-Innes way because it fits in with early teachings. I have been informed that it did not matter to those of the first G.D. Temple, Isis-Urania, because no Egyptian figures appeared on them.

a little fuller than previous designs (including Whare Ra's, which is slightly more expansive than those designs previously published). Figures 50 and 51 show 12 panels of the White Pillar, while Figures 52 and 53 show 7 panels of the Black Pillar. A number of Golden Dawn students have asked why the original plates of the Papyrus of Ani were not left intact on those designs of the English Temple's Pillars. Both Jack Taylor and Israel Regardie were of the opinion that, when the plates of the designs from the Egyptian *Book of the Dead* were matched with the 0=0, parts were left out because, in the opinion of the chiefs, they did not fully match the 0=0 in pertinent points. Figure 50, for example, is taken from a Thoth-Hermes lecture.

Panel 1. This plate shows both men and women as candidates (analogous to Ani and his wife) waiting in the antechamber of the temple before entering. They are shown playing chess, for this meaning is a subtle, hidden one. Chess is a game of strategy and thinking, hence the couple have carefully thought out the moves of deciding to enter the Order. The hawk and feather outside the anteroom represents Ament (Amentet), a Goddess of the West, the place of the setting sun and entranceway to the Hall of the Neophytes, which is synonymous with the Dwelling Place of the Dead. Ament was considered the welcomer of the dead. This whole concept, related back to the Order, shows the candidate leaving behind the old values. The bread and beer also show that nourishment will be provided on the journey of the candidate.

Panel 2. The human-headed hawks seated on the roof of the tomb relate to the two Higher Selves of the Candidates, who take their appropriate place in the Hall of the Neophytes. The figure praying beside them represents Ani (from this point on, we follow a single individual on the journey) and shows that the correct rites of initiation are being applied. The two lions back to back are Set and Tau, who support the horizon. These relate back to the two Pillars of the Temple, the entranceway to the Abode of the Blessed, which relates to the Order concept of the Unification of Osiris—our Higher Self.

Figure 50
Upper Panels of the White Pillar

Figure 51
Lower Panels of the White Pillar

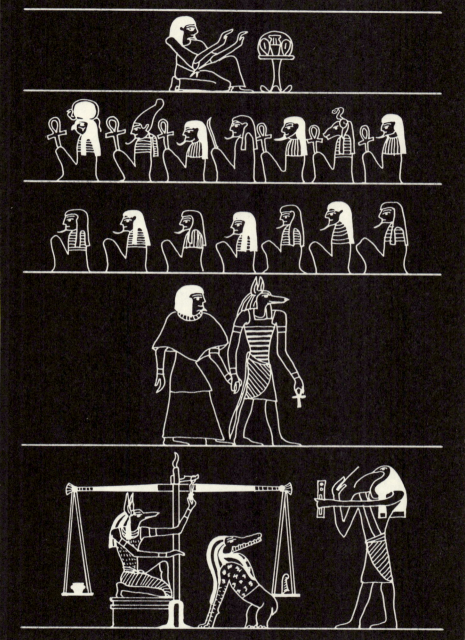

Figure 52
Upper Panels of the Black Pillar

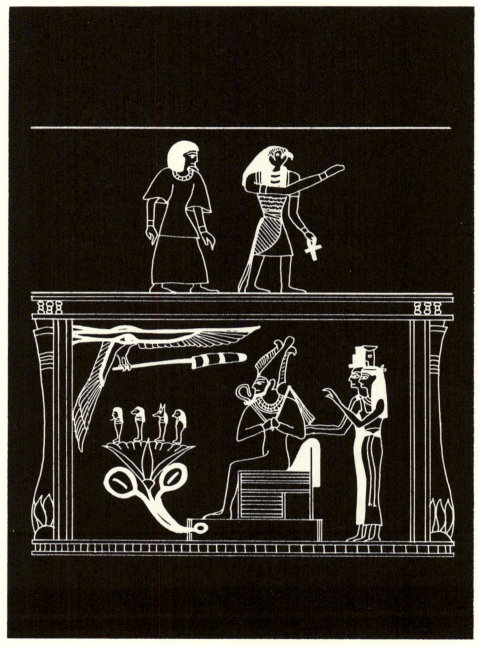

Figure 54
Lower Panel of the Black Pillar

Panel 3. Here we have the body of Ani with Nepthys at the left and Isis at the right hand side of the funeral bier, guarded by Anubis. This was called the Abode of the West. It is the point in the circumambulation where the Hiereus bars the way of the Candidate and informs him of the thin line he walks between Light and Darkness. On the far right of this plate, Ani (as the Candidate) is before Osiris (as the Hierophant), and it is his reception in the East, the first major part of the transformation, his revelation.

Panel 4. In this plate, the body of Osiris has been transformed into the Benu Bird through the purification process. The Candidate's acceptance into the Order is shown through "Khabs Am Pekht, Konx Om Pax—Light in Extension." The lotus, libation vase, and offerings on the altar represent further symbols of the transformation process as represented in Order symbology by the cross above the triangle by which the Candidate must swear in order to fully transform himself. The next aspect of this plate shows Ani lying on the bier with the forms of Nepthys and Isis (in hawk form) at each end while his Soul hovers above him with two ankhs of power. The two Urae Goddesses are also present (representing North and South). This refers to the Speech of the Hierophant and the placement of the Neophyte between the Pillars, where he is instructed in the secret signs etc. and is readied for his final consecration. The soul above him is the Higher Self advancing upwards.

Panel 5. In this place, we have Ani approaching the Water God or the final consecration of the Neophyte. The staff held by the Water God is the symbol of the year, which is the password of the Equinox. The whole process is a continuation of the soul or Higher Self of the Neophyte, which has soared upwards, passed the watchful Eye of Horus to its reception in Pools of the Two Truths, which are held together by Uatch-ura. The right-hand lake is the "Pool of Natron," while the left-hand lake is the "Pool of Salt" (another concept of the two Pillars). This shows the actions of the Higher Self in the ritual, though the Neophyte, in the physical, has not moved from the previous diagram and the actions are all on a Higher Plane. The final drawing on this plate is the Rasta, the South Gate of Anrutef, part of Herakleopolis and Northern Entrance to the Land of the Dead through which the Neophyte passes through in the circumambulation.

Panel 6. The Eye of Ra, as Osiris, over the funerary building shows the effect sunrise brought about in the 0=0 ritual by the Mystical Circumambulation in the Pathway of Light. Here the sun (which is also the soul of the Neophyte) has appeared and petitions the Guardian to give it access and strength because it is of the same substance as the gods themselves—immortal. The next figure is Thoth raising the Eye of Osiris, showing that the soul or Higher Self of the Neophyte is without blemish (this is omitted in the Brodie-Innes description of the White Pillars). The inference is that the Higher Self of the Neophyte has returned to its proper place, like the story of Thoth who overtook Set and restored the Eye to its correct place in the sky—shown as the Sky Goddess, Mehurt, Daughter of Ra and symbolic of the Heaven.

Panel 7. This shows a funeral chest with the Head of Ra, who is holding twin ankhs emerging from the pastos. It relates to Osiris as Ra partaking of himself—death and resurrection, with the four children of Horus standing by. This is the proclamation of the motto by which the Neophyte will now be known among the Order members, which relates to a rebirth.

Panel 8. The Four Canopic Gods relate to the four officers on the Dais (excluding the Hierophant), the Chiefs behind Osiris, who control the 0=0 from their thrones. Their actions have been explained previously (which was never before given to the grades of the 5=6 or below).

Panel 9. The seven gods (which are formed from the ones above) relate to the officers of the temple floor (excluding the Sentinel).

Panel 10. This plate has Two Pillars with two hawk forms between them. The hawk with the Solar Disk is Ra, while the other is Osiris. The Pillars themselves represent Tet or human sacrifice (from the cult of Tetu). Within the 0=0, this is shown when the blood is shown to the Neophyte to remind him of his oath. The next symbol, of a cat severing a snake near an acacia tree, relates to the victory of the forces of Osiris over Typhon-Set (the snake) as the last vestiges of impurity have been removed. This relates to the reverse circumambulation in the 0=0 ritual.

Panel 11. This plate shows Orisis-Ani in adoration before the god Kephera, going by in his Solar Boat. This relates to the Final Adoration in the Ritual. Kephera is a symbol of the Creator to whom the Adoration was made.

Panel 12. This shows Tem in his boat and the god Rehu in lion form. Though this plate is hard to explain at the best of times, the Order considers it the reunification with Osiris and the following of his doctrine shown by the Partaking of the Eucharist Ceremony at the end of the 0=0 ritual, where his essence is received and united with.

The Enochian Tablets and the Neophyte Ritual

The Enochian system and its association to the 0=0 ritual has been for many years something of an enigma since, in the drawing of the temple diagram, no such tablets are shown or mentioned. However, within the Inner Order, a number of papers have survived that tie the Elemental associations which compose the Enochian pyramid squares to the god-forms that rule them, and their associations to the temple officers (with the exception of the Cancellarius, Hegemon, Stolistes, and Dadouchos). What a number of students do not realize is that, while there are no Enochian Tablets indicated in the 0=0 ritual, in the permanent temples such as Isis-Urania, Bristol-Hermes, Whare-Ra, and so on, the four Tablets were left on the temple walls and were covered by a curtain the color of the element that they represented. When the Elemental grade ceremonies were done, the curtain of the particular tablet required was drawn back for the duration of the ceremony.

The curtains stifled the corporeal energies of the tablets. Their incorporeal form positively affected the ceremony, and it is this etheric energy that the temple officers drew upon. Whether Mathers originally intended this to happen is anyone's guess. Most of the early rituals were done in drawing rooms, and so on, and, more than likely, if he had so intended, the tablets would have been indicated. However, in the permanent temples, people like Jack Taylor (who held the office of Hierophant on and off for over 35 years at Whare Ra) noticed that the curtains barely stopped the etheric energies of the tablets from emanating during the 0=0 ceremony. They emanated even more so during the elemental ceremonies, when the incorporeal and corporeal energies had to be correctly balanced for the ritual to be a success. It is not our intention to involve ourselves deeply with Enochian semantics in the 0=0. However, since this book is for both Adept and Neophyte, it is impossible to separate one from the other. We would ask our readers who are not familiar with the Golden Dawn's version of the Enochian system to refer to the works of Aleister Crowley and Regardie, who have covered this subject more than adequately. The following breakdown gives the Enochian Square association to the 0=0 officers:

Enochian Squares and 0=0 Officers

Elements of Pyramid Square	God-Form	0=0 Officers
SPIRIT, or one triangle of each element	Osiris	Hierophant
WATER, or 3 out of 4 Water	Isis	Praemonstrator
EARTH, or 3 out of 4 Earth	Nepthys	Imperator
FIRE, or 3 out of 4 Fire	Horus	Hiereus
AIR, or 3 out of 4 Air	Aroueris	Past-Hierophant
2 Water, 2 Earth	Athor	Invisible Station Kerub of the East
2 Fire, 2 Water	Sothis	Invisible Station Kerub of the West
2 Air, 2 Water	Harpocrates	Invisible Station between Altar and Hegemon
2 Fire, 2 Earth	Apis	Invisible Station Kerub of the North
2 Air, 2 Earth	Anubis	Kerux
2 Fire, 2 Air	Pasht	Invisible Station Kerub of the South
Fire/Water/Earth	Ameshet	Invisible Station N.E. Child of Horus
Fire/Water/Air	Ahephi	Invisible Station S.W. Child of Horus
Earth/Water/Air	Tmoumathph	Invisible Station S.E. Child of Horus
Earth/Air/Fire	Kabexnuv	Invisible Station N.W. Child of Horus

Symbolism of the Opening

General

Within the Z.1 document, the General Exordium says:
1. The Speech in the Silence:
2. The Words against the Son of Night:
3. The Voice of Thoth before the Universe in the presence of the eternal Gods:
4. The Formulas of Knowledge:
5. The Wisdom of Breath:
6. The Radix of Vibration:
7. The Shaking of the Invisible:
8. The Rolling Asunder of the Darkness:
9. The Becoming Visible of Matter:
10. The Piercing of the Coils of the Stooping Dragon:
11. The Breaking forth of the Light:

All these are in the Knowledge of Tho-oth.

For some, the above verse may appear incomprehensible, but it is a code for breaking down the Opening of the 0=0 Ceremony. The general meaning of the above verse relates to the Great Thoth, the highest aspect of the Hermes of the most ancient Egyptian Mysteries, and corresponds almost to the Great Angel Metatron. It is the Archangel of Kether in the Briatic World. The Mercury of the Romans must not be confused with this Great Hermes. The doctrines of Gnosticism and of Valentinus approached those of the pure Kabbalah. In them, we find Speech and Silence. Across the Abyss of Silence comes the Primal Speech. The Divine Ones here referred to are the Aeons of the Atziluthic World. These formulae of knowledge are designed in terms cognizable to us in the lower world. Taking as an example, we have Eheieh, an implicit and explicit sound. "Every being pronounces its existence, the Name of the Lord of Life, by inspiration and expiration."

The Macroprosopus is Aima and Abba, Mother-Father. The two nostrils pass up and down the two breaths, as through two Great Pillars. These throw all things into vibration; compare the Rashith ha-Gilgalim. "Piercing of the Dragon's Coils" suggests the freeing of Malkuth, which is also referred to as the Washing of the Garments of the Queen, the inferior Mother. Then comes the Breaking Forth of the Light. Over Malkuth, as Guardians, are Metatron and Sandalphon, as the Two Pillars, and Nephesch ha- Messiah, the animal soul of Messiah, the Shekinah or Presence between the Kerubim.

Commentary on the General Exordium

1. The Speech in the Silence
This relates to the knock that the Hierophant gives to start the ceremony and to announce the commencement of a vibration in the Sphere of Sensation (aura) of the Candidate. This knock can be done with a stamp of the foot. Some hierophants use the base of the scepter against the throne.

2. The Words Against the Son of Night
Here we have the Cry of the Kerux, the Watcher Within, with the words "HEKAS, HEKAS, ESTE BEBELOI" (which roughly means that anyone who should not be present should get out!). The Kerux utters these words when he/she goes to the right of the Hierophant and raises his/her Wand. This is a symbol of the Ray of the Divine Light from the White Triangle of the Three Supernals, which then descends into the Darkness and warns the Evil and uninitiated to retire so that the White Triangle may be formulated upon the Altar through the combined effect of the formula of the Opening Ceremony.

3. The Voice of Thoth before the Universe in the presence of the eternal Gods

This is analogous to the opening speech of the Hierophant, where he/she asks the Kerux to check that the Hall is properly guarded, for this assures that the Portal is secure and that the energy from the current of Thoth had now manifested into the ceremony.

4. The Formulas of Knowledge

In this instance, the Hierophant calls to the Hiereus to test the members present by the "Signs of Knowledge," which shows that they, though in the Land of Blindness and Ignorance, have yet seen that the Triangle of Divine Light from the three Supernals is formulated in Darkness. You will note that the Hierophant gives the Sign of the Enterer towards the West, and it is not immediately followed by the Sign of Silence. For here the Hierophant has sent the current of Light through to the Hiereus, but he/she cannot release it (through the Sign of Silence) until it links directly into the Hiereus's throne—for then the central axis is established through Samekh and Tau. Once he/she gives the words to reawaken the images or shells of the god-forms, he/she then releases his/her current with the Sign of Silence; otherwise he/she would expend it and exhaust himself.

5. The Wisdom of Breath

It is noted that the names of the three chief officers begin with the letter "H," the letter of breath. This letter relates to its Coptic meaning, which to a certain extent is the letter H in English and can only convey its meaning in part. Taking two examples, we have Ϩ concealed in the name Osiris by the Η, the Greek capital letter *eta*. In the name Horus, it is manifest and violently aspirated, while in the name Thmaest, it is partly one and partly the other for it is compounded with the letter "T" in the Greek letter *theta*, Θ (Η, "Ae," is attributed to Chesed— Ϩ and Θ to Earth and Saturn. This is intended to affirm the Unknown Life, which is inspired from the Beyond, sent out to Aries, the commencement of the spring of the year, the life which, after being inspired, is breathed forth again. It is also the possible use of that breath, between the inspiration and the expiration, in combination between it and the forces of the microcosm.)

6. *The Radix of Vibration*

The whole is a rehearsal of the properties of the reflection of the element Air down through the Middle Pillar of the Sephiroth. It represents the reflection of Air from Kether, through Tiphareth to Yesod, and even to the citrine part of Malkuth. For the subtle Aether is, in Kether, inspired from the Divine Light beyond; thence reflected into Tiphareth, wherein it is combined with the reflexes from the alchemical principles in that great receptacle of the forces of the Tree. In Yesod, it affirms the foundation of a formula, and from Malkuth it is breathed forth or reflected back. This formula can be used by the Adept. Standing in his Sphere of Sensation, he can, by his knowledge of the sacred rites, raise himself unto the contemplation of his Yechidah and from thence aspire (in the sense of the Adspire; i.e., to attract *towards* you in breathing) downwards into himself the Lower Genius as though temporarily to inhabit himself as its temple (see Regardie's *The Middle Pillar* for a fuller explanation of this).

Another formula of vibration is hidden here. Let the Adept, standing upright, arms stretched out in the form of a Calvary Cross, vibrate a Divine Name, bringing with the formulation thereof a deep inspiration into the lungs. Let the breath be retained, mentally pronouncing the Name in the heart, so as to combine it with the forces desired to be awakened thereby; thence sending it downwards through the body past Yesod, but not resting there, but taking his or her physical life for a material basis, send it on into the feet. There momentarily formulate the Name—then, bringing it rushing upward into the lungs, thence breathe it forth strongly while vibrating that Divine Name. He or she will send the breath steadily forward into the Universe so as to awaken the corresponding forces of the Name in the Outer World. Standing with arms out in the form of a cross, when the breath had been imaginatively sent to the feet and back, bring the arms forward in "the Sign of the Enterer" while vibrating the Name out into the Universe. On completing this, make the "Sign of Silence" and remain still, contemplating the force you have invoked.

This is the secret tradition mode of pronouncing the Divine Names by vibration, but let the Adept beware that he or she applies it only to the Divine Names of the Gods. If this thing be done ignorantly in working with the Elemental or Demonic Names, the Adept may bring into himself or herself terrible forces of Evil and Obsession. The method described is called "The Vibratory Formula of the Middle Pillar."

7. *The Shaking of the Invisible*

This refers to the "Awakening of the Images—the Invisible Stations." Here the temple officers must link their Spheres of Sensations with the Invisible Images of the god-forms through the vibratory formula.

8. *The Rolling Asunder of the Darkness*

This particular phrase of the General Exordium relates to the symbolism of the Mystical Circumambulation in the Outer temple—the Macrocosm. Here we have the Procession of Officers forming in the North in readiness for the "Mystic Circumambulation in the Path of Light." This is formed in the North, beginning from the Station of Stolistes, the symbol of the Waters of Creation attracting the Divine Spirit, and therefore alluding to the Creation of the World by the Spirit and the Waters. The Order of the Mystic Circumambulation is as follows: First comes Anubis, the Watcher within. Next comes Thmaest, the Goddess of the Hall of Truth. Then comes Horus. Then comes the Goddess of the Scales of Balance. Then come the members, if the Hall be large enough, and, at the end, the Watcher Without, the Sentinel. It is as though a gigantic Wheel were revolving and expanding, as it is said: "One Wheel upon Earth beside the Kerub." The name of the Sphere of the Primum Mobile, Rashith ha-Gilgalim, signifies the heads or beginnings of whirling motions or revolutions. Of this wheel in the Mystic Circumambulation, the ascending side begins from below the Pillar of Nepthys, and the descending side from below the Pillar of Isis.

9. The Becoming Visible of Matter

The above phrase still refers to the Mystic Circumambulation, but especially to the effect of the Rise of Light in the individual. These, of course, occur simultaneously with 8, but are placed here to affirm that the subtle body centers awaken within the officers and the Candidate. Here, the auras of the officers flood with the light and power of the ceremony, which to many are quite visible. The axis of this wheel is about the Invisible Station of Harpocrates—as though that god, in the Sign of Silence, were there placed affirming the Concealment of the central Atom of the Wheel, which alone revolves not.

10. The Piercing of the Coils of the Stooping Dragon

This is best explained by referring to the Golden Dawn Lecture, "The Law of the Convoluted Revolution of the Forces Symbolized by the Four Aces Round the Northern Pole," which in turn can be related to the "Stooping Dragon Formula." This is extremely complex and was originally reserved for the Theoricus Adeptus Minor Grade, but the formula referred to above applies to the Microcosm. The Mystic Circumambulation is symbolic of the Rise of Light, and from it is drawn another formula for the circulation of the breath. It is the Formula of the Four Revolutions of the Breath (this of course does not mean the actual air inspired can be thus circulated, but only the subtle Aether which may be drawn thence, and of which it is the vehicle). This formula should be preceded by that of the Middle Pillar. By this method, having invoked the Power you wish to awaken in yourself, and contemplated it, begin its circumambulation thus: Fill the lungs and imagine the Name vibrating in the contained air. Imagine this vibration going down the left leg to the sole of the left foot—thence passing over to the soul of the right foot—up the right leg to the lungs again where it is breathed out. Do this four times to the rhythm of the Fourfold Breath.

11. The Breaking forth of the Light

The object of the Mystic Circumambulation is to attract and make the connection between the Divine Light above and the temple. Therefore, the Hierophant does not quit his/her post to take part therein, but remains there to attract, by his/her scepter, the Light from beyond the Veil. Each member, in passing, gives the Sign of the Enterer, thus projecting the Light forward on his Path from East to West, as he is the Son of Osiris and inherits the Light by birthright from him. Therefore, he goes at once to his station to fix the Light there. Thmaest, the Goddess of Truth, passes twice because her rule is of the Balance of the Two Scales, and she retires to her station between the Pillars there to complete the reflex of the Middle Column. The Watcher Within and the rest circumambulate thrice, as affirming the completion of the reflection of perfecting of the White Triangle of the Three Supernals upon the Altar. Then follows the Adoration of the God, the Vast One, the Lord of the Universe—at which again all give the Sign of the Enterer, the Sign of the Projection of the Force of Light. Only then does the Watcher declare that the sun has arisen and that the Light shineth in darkness. Now comes the battery of the 0=0 Grade—the single knock by the Hierophant which is repeated by the Hiereus and Hegemon. This affirms the establishment of the White Triangle and therefore the Completion of the Opening Ceremony. The mystic words "Khabs Am Pekht" which accompany the knocks seal the image of the Light. Their significance implies, by various Kabbalistic methods of analysis, as well as by certain reading of the Coptic and Egyptian hieroglyphics, "Light in Extension" or "May Light be extended in Abundance upon you." Konx Om Pax is the Greek corrupted pronunciation of this, put here to link the right origin.

Symbolism of the Opening—Particular

From the first knock, a current is activated in the Hierophant. This is drawn to the Hiereus, through Hegemon, then from the Dadouchos, to the Stolistes in the form of a cross with the altar as the center. This is a combination of the energy of all four crosses worn by those officers on the Dais. The Kerux, you will note, is not the recipient of any of the arms of the cross due to the fact that his/her position is not a fixed but a fluid one.

The Consecration

The consecration is an extremely precise movement pattern where, once the officers have linked the Light between them, they move in unison, like the minute hand of a clock. Each stops and starts together. You will also note that, at each position in which they consecrate it, it is done in a triad which represents the Kabbalistic Supernals of the unmanifested. The use of the first two fingers by the Stolistes when consecrating was something passed on to us from Whare Ra. It was considered quite important. The two fingers were said (by one Whare Ra Adept of 8=3 rank) to represent the Horns of the Evil One, which present a mirror image to any negativity lurking about. It is thought to nullify and confound anything of evil intent. The Dadouchos also uses these same two fingers to work the chain on the censer. Much of this, though, was a variation of the old church theme of banishment or excommunication. However, if one projects with the fingers through the Ruach it has a more effective outcome while the appropriate Name is silently vibrated in each quarter; it can clear the air very quickly. This effectiveness is based on the power of the god-form one has assumed for the duration of the ceremony.

One of the things we were taught was that, whenever possible, two people who are harmonious should take the parts of Stolistes and Dadouchos. When antagonism exists, it will ultimately come out, and usually it will play havoc with the ceremony. These two officers are controlled by the Hegemon as the tip of the triad. It is his/her duty (generally speaking, the part of Hegemon was played by a woman to help identify more quickly with the Maat principle) to link his/her aura with that of the Pillars, then from them to the Stolistes and Dadouchos while they link themselves. S/he must draw from one and give to the other (in terms of empathic energy) through the power of the Pillars. Some years ago, a friend of ours who held the office of Hegemon at Whare Ra Temple on and off over a 20-year period gave us an example of a married couple who held the offices of Stolistes and Dadouchos and who attended a ceremony just after a bitter argument. She, as Hegemon, had to try and balance their energies, which proved to be quite a formidable task for the duration of the ceremony. It has also been our experience that it is very important to check the elemental positions from a person's natal chart to see if they are suited for positions such as Stolistes and Dadouchos. The pivot of Stolistes and Dadouchos is like the half-hour position of a clock—the two officers must be directly opposite each other during the movement. The one who finishes the consecration first waits for the other to finish before moving. The published papers of Regardie show a quarter-hour position. This was changed by those at Bristol Temple.

The Circumambulation

When the Golden Dawn rituals were first penned by Mathers, the circumambulation of the Rise of Light was always circular and around the outside of the Pillars. However, as the ritual expertise developed within the Stella Matutina, a number of Adepti became aware of rings or spirals of energy emanating from the Altar. While it is true that the initiating power comes from the Hierophant's throne in the East, the Altar also generates power as well. This is one of the reasons why it is situated where it is and not in the East. By analogy, the Hierophant's throne is like a switch to turn the current on, while the Altar is analogous to the light bulb situated in the center of the room to spread light to all areas equally.

Though Adepti in the Stella Matutina (including Dion Fortune, according to Regardie) were aware of these energy rings during ritual, very little was explained in the Z documents as to why they existed when the Portal was opened in the 0=0. In New Zealand, we started experiments by tracing these patterns of energy. We found that they were not "rings" as originally thought, but spirals of exactly three and a half turns, the same number of turns as in the circumambulation. The outward reach of the spirals went as far as the Pillars, then ceased. It occurred to us to do the circumambulation *within* the Pillars instead of without, and this brought an immediate change in tempo for the whole ceremony.

The members would start off very close to the Altar, then

gradually work their way outward with each turn. Some members became very adept at detecting the spiral by tracing the energy patterns with their knee; it felt like a warm current of air or heat sensation. This was the largest modern change in the rituals by Thoth-Hermes members, though we do suggest to those readers who are active in Golden Dawn ritual to try this method for themselves and see what the results bring. The spiral, of course, in no way interferes with the basic essence of its origins but rather compliments and even transcends it.

One of the main ritual problems that Adepti of the Stella Matutina, and later the Smaragdum Thalasses, complained about was the "dead air" during the old circumambulation, as sometimes they would connect and sometimes they would not. It was found that, in the original circumambulation, the officers picked up and tried to use the last circle of the spiral. The Pillar positions became of prime importance because, at temples like Whare Ra, a little closer to the Altar than normal allowed for the final spiral from the Altar to encompass them. In cases when the Pillars were placed in the outer ring, this distorted the spirals from the Altar. Two things now became apparent. The first was that the altar size generated different size spirals. The second was that the Pillars stopped or interfered with the spirals, which were completely spent after three and a half circumambulations. If the Pillars were placed too close to the Altar, then the spirals or even the old form of the circumambulation became lopsided and emanated very erratic forms of energy. Another point of note is that the spirals took one directly over the station of the Evil One, which gave the circumambulation more control and power (which will be discussed later). The circumambulation used is shown in Figure 54.

The Particular Exordium

In the Z.1 Document, the Particular Exordium states:

1. At the Ending of the Night: At the Limits of the Light:
   Tho-oth stood before the Unborn Ones of Time!
2. Then was formulated the Universe:
3. Then came forth the Gods thereof:

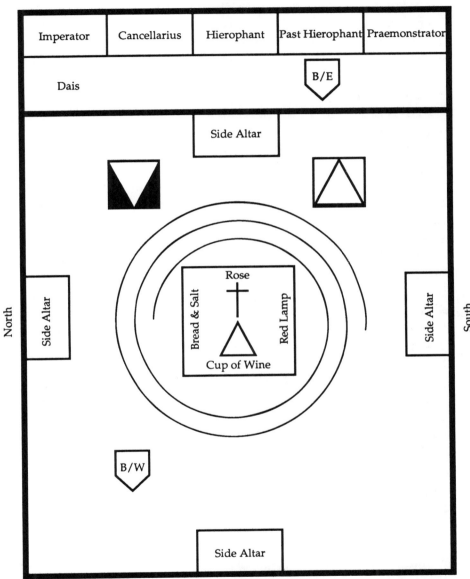

Figure 54
The Circumambulation

4. The Aeons of the Bornless Beyond:
5. Then was the Voice vibrated:
6. Then was the Name declared.
7. At the Threshold of the Entrance,
8. Between the Universe and the Infinite,
9. In the Sign of the Enterer, stood Tho-oth,
10. As before him were the Aeons proclaimed.
11. In Breath did he vibrate them:
12. In symbols did he record them:
13. For betwixt the Light and the Darkness did he stand.

The Bornless Ones of Time referred to are those coruscations of the Divine Light which are above Kether of Atziluth. In such Supernal realms, the Ain Soph, though negative to us, is there intensely positive. Thence came forth the Gods, the Voice, the Aeons, and the Name. The Egyptian Gods were generally differentiated by their Crown (for example, Amen-Ra by the feathers). Mo-oth (Maut) has the same headdress as Horus. She corresponds to the Aima Elohim. The high Hermes-Tho-oth has the same headdress as Amoun Kneph, the Sacred Spirit. Tho-oth, Truth, has two aspects—the higher and the lower. The higher is absolute; the lower is suitable to human comprehension. To tell the higher form of truth to one who cannot understand it, is to lie to him/her because, though correctly formulated, it will not be correctly received.

Applied directly to the 0=0, the Particular Exordium is the form of the ADORATION.

"Holy art Thou, Lord of the Universe!" (lines 1-2) Holy are Thou, Whom Nature hast not Formed! (lines 3-6) Holy art Thou, the Vast and the Mighty One ! (lines 7- 12) Lord of the Light and of the Darkness." (line 13)

The Adoration is done immediately after the circum-ambulation. There are three Signs of the Enterer and a Sign of Silence and these are directed towards the throne of the Hierophant. The object of this was for the Hierophant to push the Veil of Paroketh asunder with the self-contained energy in the temple, now firmly linking itself to the energy of the Second

Order through the Hierophant. The temple actually takes three phases to open correctly. The first is the knock and exchanges by the officers. The second is the circumambulation, and the third is the Adoration. At this point, the Altar is the focal point of energy, but the Adoration links the portal firmly with the powers beyond the Veil. In this instance, there are three Signs of the Enterer before the final Sign of Silence. With the Sign of the Enterer, the energy is directed at the Throne of the Hierophant, who, as Osiris, absorbs this energy coming to him/her from a balance of all officers. In this instance, he/she is just like an electrical conductor. The energy links to the officers on the floor through the Hierophant to the points beyond the Veil. The reason for the three Signs of the Enterer is that they emulate the power of the Supernals shown by the triangle on the Altar. The final Sign of Silence acts as a form of protection against any backlash of the current pushed by the Hierophant. This prevents a residue from coming back which could destroy the created portal.

With the words, "Khabs Am Pekht, Konx Om Pax—Light in Extension" the Hierophant then seals the link to the portal which the Adoration broke through to receive. As each officer knocks, the energy comes back through the Hierophant and links to them. The Kerux, Dadouchos, and Stolistes, as lesser officers, are not included. The Hegemon, for example, handles the energy of Stolistes, Dadouchos, and Kerux, as the Hegemon must regulate the energy to the other three.

To finalize this part of the ceremony, the Kerux removes the Lamp, Rose, Cup, and Paten of bread and salt from the Altar (see Figures 55 through 59). Starting at the East and moving in a clockwise direction, these items work together on many different levels. In their more basic form, they represent the organs of the body of the deceased and are placed in the four directions with the organs of the alimentary system (the most material and earthy) in the North, those of the circulatory system in the South, the receptive system in the East (the Source of Life and Light), and the organs that cast out in the West (which borders on the Qlippoth). The relationship to these bodily organs may appear at first glance to be symbolic, but they are actually worked on

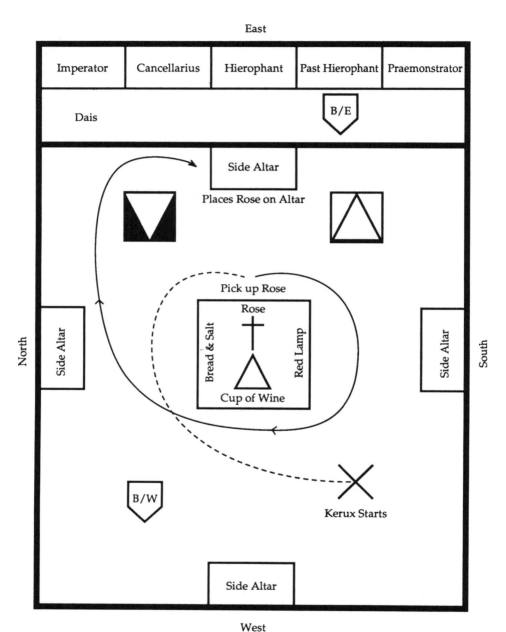

Figure 55
Circumambulation of the Kerux — Beginning

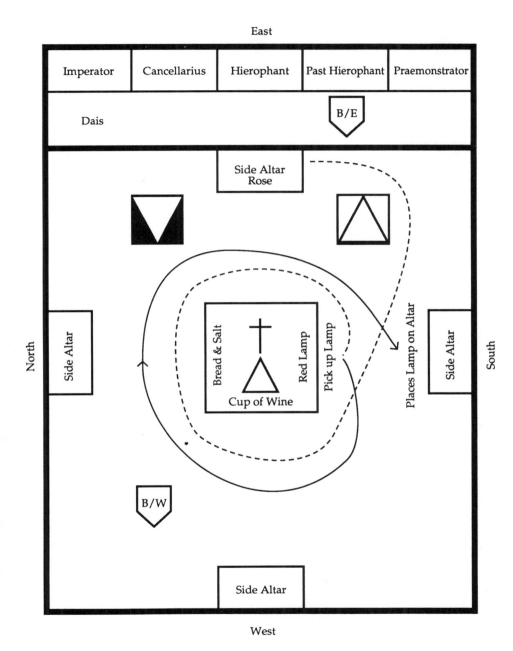

Figure 56
Circumambulation of Kerux from East to South

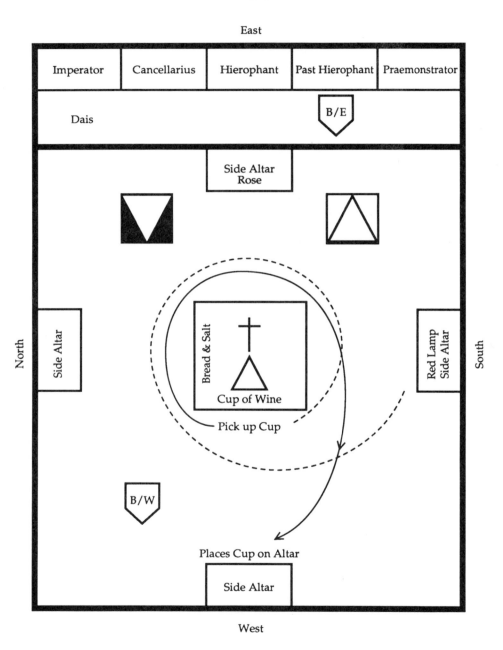

Figure 57
Circumambulation of the Kerux from South to West

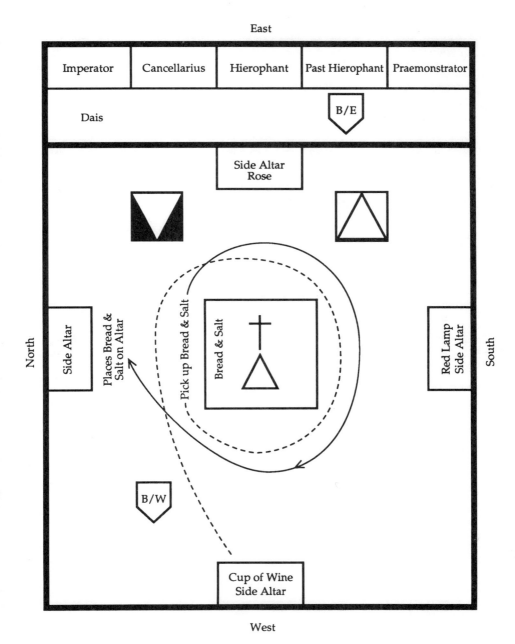

Figure 58
Circumambulation of the Kerux from West to North

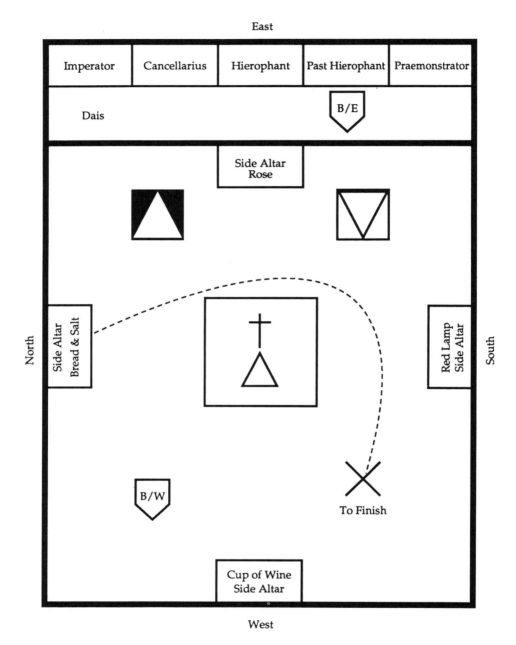

Figure 59
Cikrcumambulation of the Kerux — Finish

through the magnetized process of ritual. Dion Fortune, in her book *Psychic Self Defense,* claimed that the 0=0 ritual she experienced actually repaired her vitality. Many others have made similar claims here in New Zealand and in England. When the implements are taken from the Altar, the corresponding process taking part in the Candidate is fundamentally one of removal—of the etheric blockages in the aura, so that it becomes attuned to that of the ceremony; for the Candidate is controlled by the temple officers long before he or she enters the Hall. The current that they work under is the Osirian one, through the imagery of the Hall of the Two Truths, for this allows the Order access to the Higher Self, who must stand apart from the Candidate, during part of the ceremony. Taylor often stated that the placement of the implements is vital to the success or failure of the ceremony. Not only must they be placed in their respective directions, but they must link correctly to the God-forms that they represent as well. Though the Canopic Gods are in the corners of the Hall, it must be remembered that they cover an entire area, between each cardinal point, and thus are placed centrally between the two.

The spirals initiated by the Kerux are extremely important, for, when done correctly, they draw the power from the central Altar and link it to the cardinal points. This is not to be confused with the actions of the circumambulation which gives the Rise of Light. This is distinctly different, as the circumambulation allows the Light, or the current vibrational pitch, to enter the body of the officers, stimulate the etheric body of the Candidate, and help open the temple. The spirals expand the consciousness of the Candidate through the Osirian current or influence so that the symbolic parts of the Candidate can be removed correctly and without damage. Taylor quoted a case where the Kerux at Whare Ra, during one 0=0 ceremony, accidently dropped the Paten in the South. After the ceremony, the Neophyte had an inflamed intestinal disorder that was a mystery to the doctors. When Felkin heard of this, he did a small ceremony involving the replacement of the Paten, and, within an hour after the ceremony, the intestinal pain and disorder ceased.

Apart from the etheric influences directly on the body of the Candidate, the implements on the Altar represent the component parts of the Ruach, analogous to the Will (Rose), Memory (Cup), Reason (Paten & Salt), Desire (Lamp), and Imagination as the component part which holds all together (the Altar). This is the start of the dismantling of the bondage that the Ruach has over the Candidate and allows the Light of the Neshamah to illuminate the mind.

Symbolism of the Admission
of the Candidate

Preparation of the Candidate

The Candidate is waiting without the Portal under the care of the Sentinel—"The Watcher Without"—that is, under the care of the form of Anubis of the West, symbolically called that so that he[1] may keep off the "Dog-Faced Demons," the opposers of Anubis, who rise from the confines where matter ends to deceive and drag down the soul. The Ritual of the 31st Path says:

> ... since, ever dragging down the Soul and leading it from the Sacred Things, from the confines of Matter arise the terrible Dog-faced Demons, never showing a true image unto mortal gaze.

The real link of the Candidate, with the Order, comes through his or her application to join the Order. This fine etheric thread becomes the link, with the Candidate, that enables the subtle centers to be manipulated by the ceremony going on within the main Hall.

The Hegemon, the representative of the Goddess of Truth and Justice, superintends the preparation and symbolism. She is the Presider of the Equilibrium and administrates the process of

---

[1]Throughout this chapter, the masculine pronoun is used in its generic sense to indicate either sex.

159

equilibrium in the Candidate himself through the symbols of rectitude and self-control.

The actual preparation of the Candidate should be performed by the Sentinel—the "Watcher Without"—to insure that this preparation is accomplished so that the establishment of equilibrium can occur. Therefore, the Hegemon superintends the preparation rather than actually performs it.

A triple cord is bound around the body of the Neophyte, symbolizing the binding and restriction of the lower nature. It is triple in reference to the White Triangle of the three Supernals.

The eyes are bandaged to symbolize that the Light of the material world is but Darkness and illusion compared with the radiance of the Divine Light. The preparation also represents a certain temporary binding and restriction of the natural body.

The Candidate's Entrance into the Hall

The single knock given by the Hegemon outside the door represents the consenting will of the natural human to receive the force formulated by the Hierophant. It is answered by the Kerux inside, as if a witness were confirming the same. This being done, the Kerux, as a witness, demands authority from the Hierophant to admit the Candidate into the Hall of Truth and Justice. The Hierophant, granting permission, seals the Candidate's aura with a new name given to the physical body of the outward man but signifying the aspirations of its soul.

When the Candidate enters the Hall (normally from the West), he becomes a cornerstone of a triangle. The Hegemon is opposite and level with him. The Sentinel is behind them making up the tip of the triangle. At this juncture, it is important to remember that the Portal of the ceremony does not stretch to the four walls of the Hall, but rather resembles a spherical shape. The exact size of it depends on the Hall, but there are normally quite a few feet around the edge where members not taking part sit and view the ceremony. In front of the triangle, without the Portal, an identical triangle just inside the Portal is formed by the Kerux, Stolistes, and Dadouchos, as shown in Figure 60.

The Portal becomes the separating point between the two

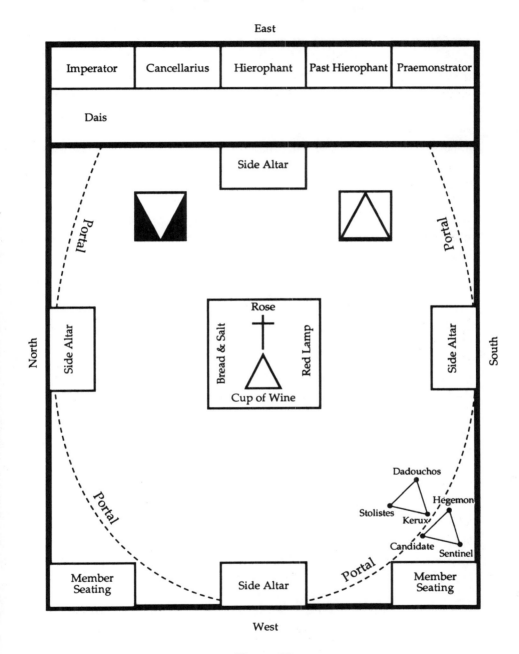

Figure 60
Entrance of the Candidate

triangles. Particular attention must be made to the rim of the Portal, for no officer is to go outside it. To breach the Portal during the ceremony opens it to negative influences. Crossing over from one side to the other must be done correctly. The Hegemon is the only one who can do this during the ceremony, because she is another one of the forms of Maat, part of the basic essence of the formulation of the Hall itself. One can only ascertain exactly where the Portal is through experience, though in practice it is easily found and detected by a heat sensation that is usually about 12 inches in diameter.

To bring the Candidate over the Portal, the Hegemon must first have him consecrated while he stands on the band of the Portal itself. This alters his already attuned aura so that it will balance with the energy within the Portal.

The Kerux instantly bars the Candidate's passage to mark that, though he has been admitted, the natural human being of unpurified desires cannot be a dweller in the Hall of Truth. The consecration immediately calls into action the Pillars of the Candidate's own Sphere of Sensation. This is the first of four consecutive consecrations because, when the Pillars of the Tree are projected onto the Sphere of Sensation, there are four Pillars, of which the Middle Pillar is the axis. The external Pillars represent the boundaries of the aura. The central Pillar represents the subtle body centers, or the minor chakras, situated on the front of the body (these are grouped Kabbalistically), but the main seven chakras are not directly stimulated.

The Hegemon uses her Ruach to stimulate that of the Candidate. At this point in the ceremony, the astral appearance of the Candidate is that of a form wrapped in Darkness, as if extinguished thereby, and having unto his right, and unto his left, the faint semblance of the two Great Pillars of Fire and of Cloud from which issue faint rays into the Darkness which covers him.

Immediately above his Sphere of Sensation, there will appear a ray of bright Light, as if preparing to penetrate the Darkness covering him. The result of this will be that the Candidate, during the whole Ceremony of Admission, will usually appear to be somewhat automatic and vague. This is not unlike the Indian guru helping a student by giving him some energy so that certain blockages can be removed, but on a much lower scale.

The break in the Portal, caused as both the Candidate and the Hegemon cross over, is held in check by the Kerux with the help of the Stolistes and Dadouchos, who use their energy to focus on closing the opening after the crossing.

Another point of significance is also made apparent by the Candidate, dressed in black, representing the dark untrodden Path, and the Hegemon, in white, representing the illuminated way. The Candidate and the Hegemon enter the darkest part of Malkuth and they walk to the Lightest part, citrine. The doctrine is that, in Malkuth, there are four Kabbalistic Trees of Life, each related to a letter of YHVH—or simply the Four Worlds applied to Malkuth. The Candidate must go from the Malkuth of Assiah (Heh) to Malkuth of Atziluth (Yod).

Now the Hegemon, throughout the ceremony, acts as a guide, prompter, and answerer for the Candidate. Her office with regard to the Candidate is analogous to that of the Candidate's Higher Soul—wherefore also the Hegemon holds in her hand the miter-headed scepter, to attract, since it is the Scepter of Wisdom, the Higher Self of the Candidate.

At this moment, as the Candidate stands before the Altar, as the simulacrum of the Higher Self is attracted, so also arises the form of the Evil Persona of the Candidate—and were it not for the power of the 42 lettered name in the Palaces of Yetzirah (the gods of which name being usually called the "Great Assessors of Judgment"), the actual Evil Persona would at once formulate and be able to obsess the Ruach of the Candidate. For, seeing that at this time the simulacrum of the Higher Soul is attracting the Neschamah of the Candidate, the human will is not as powerful in the Ruach for the moment because the Aspirant of the Mysteries is now divided. That is, his Neschamah is directed to the contemplation of his Higher Self, attracted by the Hegemon. His natural body is bound and blinded, his Ruach threatened by the simulacrum of the Evil Persona attracted by Omoo-Szathan, and a species of shadow of himself thrown forward to the place of the Pillars, where the Scales of Judgment are set. At the same time that the first consecration establishes a semblance to the Pillars on his right and left, it also has drawn forth from him a semblance of himself to the place vacated by the Hegemon between the Pillars.

Here, then, stands the shadow of the Candidate while the Scales of the Balance oscillate unseen. Unseen and colossal, there is imaged before him Tho-oth, as Metratron, in the Sign of the Enterer of the Threshold. He is ready, according to the decision of the human will, to permit or withhold the descent of the Lower Genius of the Candidate.

The Obligation of the Candidate

The Obligation of the Candidate has three major functions. The most obvious one is towards the preservation of the Order's anonymity through secrecy. The next level is the binding process that submits the Candidate as part of the new-found Order, which in many ways is a form of esoteric discipline. The final, and deepest phase, is the action or effect the Obligation has on the Candidate through the actions of the Ruach.

When the right hand is placed within the triangle on the Altar, the Ruach is then controlled by the Will—through the operation of Geburah (through Elohim Gibor and the Archangel Kamael), and the vibration of this Sephirah within the Candidate. The Will, under this Archangel's direction, then helps with the force to which the Candidate has bound himself. In simple terms, the Will acts as a type of subconscious police force.

Now a great deal has been said of the Golden Dawn Neophyte Obligation. Taylor taught us that an Oath such as this was in reality up to the dictates of one's own conscience. Some have considered the Obligation as a symbol of the Lightning Flash coming down the Tree of Life, which descends into the aura, but, in effect, no such thing happens. The Obligation binds the Candidate to his Higher Self. As Aleister Crowley put it, the Obligation affirms the very existence of the devotee, and that is inherent in our survival instincts; i.e., not to put ourselves at anyone's mercy whether the person be in the Order or not. The

Obligation activates man's affirmation of his existence, as linked with a form that is beyond the sense of the self to fully comprehend, thus pushing it deep into the layers of the self.

Clairvoyant observation of the Candidate during the Oath shows that a red ray of Geburah is produced in the Sphere of Sensation of the Candidate. This is a combination of fear and martial discipline. The Obligation of the Neophyte uses the will, through the faculty of the imagination, to link other parts of the Ruach together. Also, when the Obligation is taken, the Higher Self stands in the Station of Harpocrates, the God of Silence, whose form is to protect the Candidate from the Evil One in front of him. Once this silence is broken, the Evil One can then take over as the protection of Harpocrates is withdrawn.

Meanwhile, the Great Assessors of Judgment examine the truth of the accusations formulated by the evil and averse antithesis. The Assessors of Judgment come not under the head of the Invisible Stations, but, during the Obligation and Circumambulation of the Candidate, until he is brought to the Light, they hover immediately about the limits of the Portal, with their evil antithesis immediately below. Therefore, when the Candidate stands before the Altar prior to the Obligation, the decision is actually taken by the human will of the Candidate. He sees a disintegration of his component parts. The process of symbolic judgment takes place during the speech of the Hierophant to the Candidate, the answer of the Hegemon, and the Candidate's consent to take the Obligation.

The moment the Candidate consents, the Hierophant advances between the Pillars as if to assert that the judgment is concluded. He advances by the Invisible Station of Harpocrates to that of the Evil Triad. He symbolically stomps down so that, as Aroueris, he stands upon the opposer. He then comes to the East of the Altar, interposing between the place of the Evil Triad and the Candidate. At the same time, the Hierophant advances on the Candidate's left. The Hegemon, on his right, formulates about him the symbol of the Higher Triad before she places his hand upon the symbol of the Three Supernals lying upon the Altar. Again, before doing so, he has been bidden to kneel in adoration of that symbol, as if the natural man abrogated his will before the Divine Consciousness.

As he kneels in the presence of the Triad of Aroueris, Thmaa-est, and Horus, he places his left hand in that of his initiator to affirm his passive reception of the ritual. His right hand is on the white triangle as a symbol of his passive aspiration towards his Higher Self. His head is bowed to represent the voluntary submission of the human will to the divine—and for this latter reason he repeats in the Obligation his name in the Outer World.

A very important part of the Obligation is the use of the sword by the Hiereus. In the hands of an untrained officer, more harm than good can be caused. This is yet another reason for the temple officers on the floor to be all Inner Order members.

There were at least three people at Whare Ra Temple that had their clairvoyant abilities removed after the sword touched the nape of the neck. One person who could see auras to a high degree lost this ability immediately and was told by his Seniors that it would come back better than before—something which did not happen. Twenty years later, another identical case occurred. Taylor recalled its happening a number of times. Since the discipline at Whare Ra regarding excellence was quite strict, one can only come to the conclusion that the officer of Hiereus had not performed his function correctly, in the field of magnetic manipulation, at this vital moment in the ceremony. While a few lost clairvoyant abilities, quite a number gained them; and, as the sword of the Hiereus was placed at the nape of the neck, a distinct click could be heard by those around the Candidate. This was usually considered a sign that this part of the ceremony had been done well.

Taylor maintained that a good Hierophant should always meet the Candidate informally and study his aura to see if there were any abnormalities in it so that incidents of lost clairvoyance could be avoided. In one incident recalled by Taylor, he actually refused to do a 0=0 ceremony because he read indicators of mental imbalance in the Candidate's aura. (This caused quite a stir at the time.) The individual was put through some time later by another Hierophant, and Taylor's predictions proved correct some months later when the individual was placed in psychiatric care. When individuals showed natural clairvoyant abilities during the Obligation, Taylor would always reinforce the Candidate's aura with his own magnetism to prevent the incorrect use of the sword in the hands of an inexperienced Hiereus.

The Hierophant gives one knock, affirming that the submission unto the Higher Self is perfect. Only at this moment does the invisible and colossal figure of Tho-oth cease to be in the Sign of the Enterer and give the Sign of Silence, permitting the first real descent of the Genius of the Candidate, who descends to the Invisible Station of Harpocrates as a witness of the Obligation.

The Hiereus and the Hierophant return to their thrones, and therefore it is not Aroueis, but Osiris himself, that addresses the speech to the Candidate—"The Voice of My Higher Self," etc., which confirms the link established between the Neschamah and the Genius by formulating the conception thereof into the Ruach. For this, Osiris speaks in the character of the Higher Soul, the symbolic form of which is standing between the columns before him. The affirmation of the Higher Soul as the god of the human being does not mean that this is the only God. Rather, it indicates that it is the only presentiment of Him which the natural human being can grasp at all. Neither is it just to say that the Higher Soul is one with God, seeing that the part is by no means the whole; nor can the whole be accurately and sufficiently described as an assemblage of parts. Let not the reverence for the God of thy self cause thee by a misconception to lose thy reverence for the Gods who live forever—the Aeons of Infinite Years. Herein is a great error, and one which may, in its ultimatum, bring about the fall of the genius. This is a sin which entails none the less terrible consequences because it is a sign of the Higher Plane, where the choice is not between good and evil but between the lower and higher forms of good.

The Circumambulation of the Candidate

In the first spiral of the Circumambulation, knocks are given in the East and West only. The concept here is to instill in the Candidate a sense of equilibrium, for those knocks which signify the Middle Pillar of balance represent the central axis of the Tree of Life in the ceremony. More importantly, though, it activates the realization of the Middle Pillar within the body of the Candidate himself. This subtlety teaches the Candidate focalization (this form of awareness was never intended to be instantaneous, but should develop over the ensuing months between the Neophyte and the Zelator grade). Therefore, the Mystic Circumambulation in the Path of Darkness led by the Kerux with symbolic Light formulates the Higher Soul, which is not the only Divine Light, but rather a spark from the Ineffable Flame. The Kerux, in his turn, is but the Watcher of the Gods.

After the Kerux comes the Hegemon, the translator of the Higher Self, leading the Candidate. Then come the Goddesses of the Scales of the Balance, the Stolistes and the Dadouchos. They move once round; the formation in the Darkness of the Binah angle of the White Triangle of the Three Supernals. The Hierophant knocks once as they pass him, in affirmation of Mercy—the Hiereus in affirmation of Severity; and the invisible Assessors each give the Sign of the Enterer as the Candidate passes on the way. At the second passing of the Hierophant, the knock affirms the commencement of the angle of Chokmah.

The first barring of the Candidate, on the second spiral, by the Kerux, is extremely important, for while he bars the gateway to the West, he actually does so in the South. This represents a further division of the spiral. The red (Shin) part of the Kerux's wand is placed firmly in the Candidate's Tiphareth center, working directly through his Ruach to stimulate and attract the current of the Chiah into direct operation. To perform this function correctly, it cannot be done by someone in the Outer Order (yet another argument for Inner Order members for temple floor officers). The Kerux, according to the Z.3, uses his Magic Staff of Power to represent a ray of Divine Light which kindles the Hidden Fire. The Red Ray of the Kerux, through his

Ruach, goes through directly to the Ruach of the Candidate by the power of the fiery part of the Wand. The Kerux Grips the Wand in the yellow (airy) band. This shows that he is in control of his own Ruach; then he directs it to the Chiah by the power of the Secret Fire.

The caduceus lamen that he wears also has a part to play which goes beyond mere symbolism. Its function is to balance the energy directed by the Kerux, and it is placed directly over the Kerux's Tiphareth center, analogous to his Ruach. Any emotive force of a disruptive nature is held in check by this. Also it controls the amount of energy with which the Candidate is stimulated.

The consecration by Fire and Water is more than a simple consecration. The positioning of these officers in relationship to the Candidate is always in the form of a triangle.

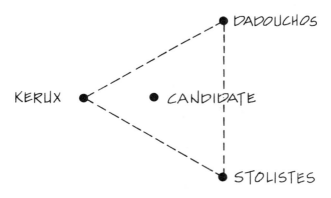

Figure 61
The Barring of the Candidate

The barring is shown in Figure 61. Figure 62 shows the Consecration by Fire.

The Kerux retains his position while the Stolistes and Dadouchos move up together so they are both alongside the Candidate. Then they turn 180 degrees to face him, still maintaining the triangular position around him. During the consecration by Fire, the Dadouchos slightly turns the Candidate towards her, but not enough to disrupt the pressure of the

Kerux's wand. The Stolistes then repeats a similar action when purifying by Water. Apart from the practical considerations, this slight turning is also to instill the concept that, no matter which way the Candidate is turned, the pressure of resistance is still applied to him. Realizing that he has no way to go but ahead, the Candidate must surrender himself to his guides who represent, by reflection, the White Triangle of the Supernals on the Altar. They represent the three phases of his Soul to guide him on the Pathway of Light.

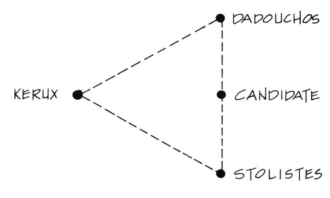

Figure 62
The Consecration by Fire

When the Candidate reaches the Throne of the Hiereus, he is then barred a second time. The regular challenge is part of the Current of Horus (note that the central lines from the temple floor is mainly under the influence of Horus, East to West.) Here, the Hiereus confronts the soul of the Candidate with the negative forces present within the self. These are Qlippothic in origin and must be faced by recognizing their existence, for not to do so allows them to take over aspects of our own natures. What has happened here is that the Hiereus, in this instance, represents the archetype of these forces. His sword is placed about six inches in front of the Candidate's Tiphareth center and as such threatens his Ruach. The Hiereus projects an image of foreboding at the Candidate. The flat of the sword being held in this barring position, the Hiereus vibrates the energy of the Qlippothic force (which he guards) and which the Candidate is able to recognize so that, when he encounters this force again, he can withdraw from it.

The second consecration is designed to rid the Candidate of the Qlippothic forces to which he was exposed. The Hiereus must try to project fear of these elements to the Candidate—which, frankly, takes a good deal of effort. It is done through the Will of the Ruach, directed through the red (Geburah) part of the sword and centralized with the Tiphareth center of the Hiereus.

There are a number of ways to do this, but the simplest way is for the Hiereus to encase his aura with the red ray of Geburah by vibrating "Elohim Gibor." This is generally done when the Candidate is barred at the South. As the Candidate is ushered towards the West, he then directs the energy through the sword and vibrates "YHVH ALOAH VE-DAAS," so that a red (Geburah) and gold (Tiphareth) magnetic influence are present. It is this combination that emanates to the Ruach of the Candidate so that he can sense the Qlippothic forces in the future.

The next barring of the Candidate is at the North—the gateway to the East. At this point, the Candidate is not initially touched by the Kerux but is halted by the Hegemon, using arm pressure. The Kerux merely waves his wand in front of the Candidate by the center band. This action also lightly touches the Ruach of the Candidate before the final post in the East is reached. Here, the Candidate has reached the point analogous to Binah, which in itself relates to the Neshamah, which is then stimulated through the Mem part of the wand of the Kerux.

The next barring and consecration of the Candidate is an extension of the previous one and the commencement of the formulation of the angle of Kether. The hoodwink is again slipped up, giving a still further glimpse of the nature of the Divine Light, though, to the mind of the Candidate, an imperfect one. Therefore it is to him, as expressed in the answer of the Hegemon, a Light dimly seen through the Darkness, yet heralding a glory beyond. The speech of the Hierophant then formulates the forces of the hidden central Pillar.

The Sealing of the Candidate's Aura

After the Circumambulation, the Candidate passes to the Altar of the Universe, which receives the influences of the three Pillars. It should be as though the ray from the Divine would descend into the darkness of the mind, for then, but not until then, is he fitted to realize what are the first things necessary to the "Search for the Shining Light."

As the Hierophant advances along the Path of Samekh, he represents the Divine Light coming through the Ruach of the Candidate. He pauses briefly between the Pillars, and his form is stabilized by the Goddess of the Scales, as she also represents the Holy Guardian Angel (a title sometimes analogous to the Tarot Trump "Temperance" in its archetypal representation), the perfected man. When the Hierophant reaches Yesod, he again pauses. Here the Hierophant, as the descending Light of the Order, enters the Candidate's Nephesch through a direct magnetic link. As he stands on the station of the Evil One, he takes control of the Nephesch and pushes aside any negativity, so that the Light draws in the Light from above to the Candidate while the Banner of the East reflects it in the temple (Figure 63).

The form of Harpocrates now formulates a protective envelope around the Candidate, which draws forth the Higher Self of the Candidate, for the negative influences (now under the control of the Hierophant) cannot harm it. The Hierophant gives a single knock to seal the matter and then invokes the Lord of the Universe. Then only is the hoodwink removed. The Hierophant, Hiereus, and Hegemon join scepters and sword above the Candidate's head, thus formulating the Supernal Triad, and assert his reception into the Order. They then recite the mystic words to seal the current of the Flowing Light. This is the point where the magnetic influences of the three officers work together, and they direct their influence to the aura of the Candidate. The energy of each implement vibrates so that, at this point, a triangle of Light can be seen (clairvoyantly) above the Candidate's head. This is brought to a fine point with the words "KHABS AM PEKHT—KONX OM PAX—LIGHT IN EXTENSION."

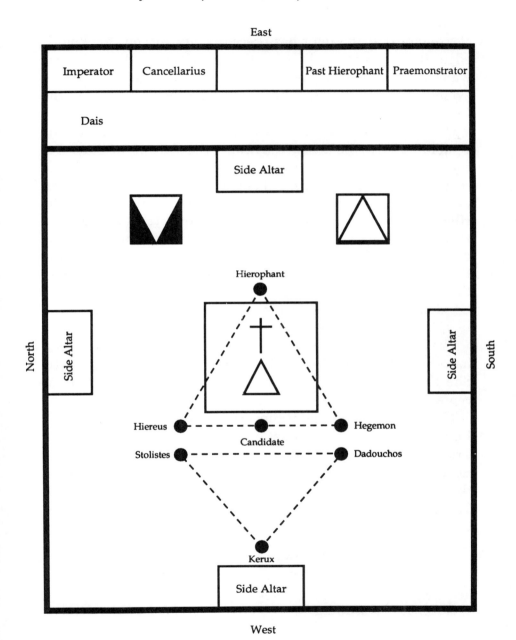

Figure 63
Sealing the Aura of the Candidate

The Hierophant now calls forward the Kerux, cautioning the Candidate that the light has preceded him without his knowledge. It represents to him here a vague formulation of ideas which as yet he can neither grasp nor analyze. This light is not a symbol of the Higher Self, but a ray from the Guardians of the Order themselves.

Only after having thus been brought to the Light is the Candidate led to the East of the Altar—the place of the Station of the Evil Triad—to affirm that with this Light, he will be able to cast out and trample on his Evil Persona, which, when it has been put in its place, will then become a support to him. It is to the Hiereus, "Avenger of the Gods," therefore, that the duty of entrusting the Candidate with the Secret Signs and so on is delegated. It is he who places him for the first time between the Pillars and superintends his final consecration—thus bringing the peculiar force handled by the Hiereus to the aid of the Candidate so that he may more safely and resolutely combat the temptations of the Evil Persona.

The Hierophant has returned to his throne while the Hegemon holds the insignia of the Hiereus while he confers the Signs, etc. She thus affirms to the Candidate the necessity of the force represented by the Hiereus.

The Hierophant on the throne, the Hiereus East of the Black Pillar, and the Hegemon East of the White Pillar again form a Triad, which here represents the reflection of the Three Supernals. The Higher Soul is formulated between the Pillars in the Place of Equilibrium. The Candidate is in the place of the Evil Triad, and the Hiereus now advances to the place of Harpocrates between the Pillars to give the words.

The Instruction of the Candidate

The symbolism and meaning of the Step, Signs, Grip, or Token, and the Words have a threefold interpretation:

1. Apparent meaning.
2. Spiritual or mystical reference.
3. Practical application.

Each is therefore considered under three headings.

First, the foot is advanced about six inches. This represents the foot on the side of Chesed being put forward and taking a hesitating step in Darkness. The left foot is used to represent the power of Isis, or the beginning of action, rather than Nepthys as the end thereof. The distance of "six inches" is employed here only to render it more intelligible to modern initiates. It means a convenient measure of six, and preferably six times the measure of the phalanx of the thumb—the Spirit and Will.

Second, it symbolizes the beginning of the stamping down of the Evil Persona. The foot is advanced six metrical distances, answering to the number six of Tiphareth—Osiris—alluding therefore to the self-sacrifice necessary to accomplish this.

Third, it represents the practical application of the beginning of a magical force. Let the Adept, in using the Sign of the Enterer, give the step as he commences the Sign and let him take that step as if he stamped upon the Earth, and the Earth quaked and rocked beneath him. As it is said, "Clouds and Darkness are round about Him—Lightnings and thunders the Habitation of His feet." Its secret name is "The Step of the Avenger."

Saluting Sign

1. That of groping forward in search of truth.

2. It represents the involution and bringing forward of the Light into the material to aid the will of the Candidate in his search for and aspiration towards the Higher.

3. Standing as before described, in the form of the god, and elevating the mind to the contemplation of Kether, take the step like a stroke with the foot, bring the arms up above the head as if touching the Kether, and as the step is completed bring the hands over the head forward. Thrust them out directly and horizontally from the level of the eyes—arms extended, fingers straight, palms downward, the hands directed toward the object it is wished to charge or to affect. At the same time, sink the head till the eyes look exactly between the thumbs. In this way, the rays from the eyes, from each finger, and from the thumb must all converge upon the object attacked. If any of them disperse, it is a weakness.

Thus performed, this Sign is a symbol of tremendous attacking force and of projection of will power, and it should be employed in all cases where force of attack is required—especially in charging talismans and the like. Generally, it is best to have the thumbs and all the fingers extended—but if a particular effect is desired, you may extend only the fingers appropriate thereto, keeping the rest folded back in the hand. Herewith also may be combined the attribution of the planets to head (Mars to the right nostril, Mercury to the mouth, etc., as explained in the Microcosm lecture), sending at the same time an imaginary ray of color of the planet desired from the part of the head attributed to it. But, when finished, be careful to withdraw the rays again or they will remain like so many outlets of astral force and thus exhaust you. The best way to protect yourself against this is to give the Sign of Silence immediately. For the first Sign should always be answered by the second. The secret names of the Saluting Sign are "the Attacking Sign" or "the Sign of the Enterer of the Threshold."

The Sign of Silence

1. This is simply that of secrecy regarding the Mysteries.

2. It is the affirmation of the station of Harpocrates, wherein the Higher Soul of the Candidate is formulated in part of the admission ceremony. It is the symbol of the center and of the "Voice of the Silence," which answers in secret the thought of the heart.

3. The Sign of Silence withdraws the force put out by the Sign of the Enterer. Take upon thyself as before taught the colossal figure of the god, Harpocartes. Bring the left foot sharply back, both heels together. Beat the ground once with the left foot as it is placed beside the right. Bring the left hand to the mouth and touch the center of the lower lip with the left forefinger. Close the other fingers and thumb and drop the right hand to the side. Imagine a watery vapor encircles you. This is the reflux of the current.

This Sign is also used as protection against attack. The Sign represents a concentration of astral Light about the person.

Having given the Sign as above, it is a protection against all attack and danger of obsession. To make it stronger, the form of the god should be taken. If spiritual force is required, formulate as if standing on a lotus or rising from it. For force in contemplation and meditation, formulate as if seated upon a lotus. But for more material force, imagine standing upon a dragon or a serpent like some statues of Harpocrates. As a defense and protection, the Sign is as strong as the Banishing Pentagram, though different in nature. And as the Sign of the Enterer represents attack, so does this Sign represent defense thereto, as a Shield is a defense against the Sword. From this Sign is a formula of invisibility derived. There is a story told by Dr. Edmund William Berridge, who was a prominent member of the Golden Dawn:

> A few years ago I noticed that invariably after a prolonged interview with a certain person I felt exhausted. At first I thought it only the natural result of a long conversation with a prosy, fidgety old gentleman, but later it dawned upon me that being a man of exhausted nervous vitality, he was really preying upon me. I don't suppose that he was at all externally conscious that he possessed a vampire organism, for he was a benevolent, kind-hearted old man who would have shrunk in horror from such a suggestion. Nevertheless, he was, in his inner personality, an intentional vampire, for he acknowledged that he was to marry a young wife in order, if possible, to recuperate his exhausted system. The next time, therefore, that he was announced, I closed myself to him before he was admitted. I imagined that I had formed round myself a complete investure of odic fluid, surrounding me on all sides but not touching me, and impenetrable to any hostile currents. This magical process was immediately and permanently successful—I never had to repeat it.

The "odic fluid" that Dr. Berridge mentions is the same as "an encircling and enclosing watery vapor." This may be done effectively in the astral as well as physically.

The Secret Names of this Sign are "The Sign of the God of Silence" or the "Sign of Defense or Protection." It may be performed with any finger of either hand, but it is most protective when the left forefinger is used, the Water of Chesed, for the fingers of the right hand represent more violent action, and those of the left more watery action. With regard to taking on mentally the forms of the gods, it may be here noted that the process is of great assistance and use in all magical workings, whether of invocation or evocation, contemplation, meditation, skying in the spirit vision, alchemy, and so on. For the forms of the gods do here represent a certain symbolic material action of the divine forces.

The Sign of the Silence is done after the Sign of the Enterer because it stops the force one activates with the initial Sign. The reason that three Signs are done is to build up more power, but they are all always stopped when the Sign of Silence is given.

During the Circumambulation, when the Sign of the Enterer is given, it is to a certain extent a blind force, for here the energy is expended out only to fortify the outward spiral (under the old regime, it was the circle; going outside the Pillars the same principle was applied) and the energy here expended emanating through the aura as the individual goes around the Altar, but is not given a boost or directed until one arrives at the throne of the Hierophant. The Sign of Harpocrates, given straight after it, seals this force back into your aura so no leakages can occur. This is done a number of different ways, though the Invisible Station of Harpocrates is its power source. For this is where the first Circumambulation is done, nearest the Altar, and it expands out with every turn.

In our own training in the Sign of Silence and its uses, Taylor gave us an example of an individual who did the Sign of the Enterer, and, during the Circumambulation, had energy leaking out of him like a sieve (which Taylor observed through his remarkable clairvoyant ability). This was only rectified when the Sign of Silence was done. Taylor later found that the individual had suffered a personal loss that same day, but had decided to do the ceremony to gain strength from it.

It should be pointed out here that the temple members observing the ceremony, but not taking part in it, should join in the Circumambulation of the temple officers. The Sign of Silence is done in the Astral Form of Harpocrates from its original position. The power of this god-form draws out towards the East, pulled there by the *kavanah,* or "intent," of the first Circumambulation. The other times it is done, this god-form expands and pushes along the spiral of the Circumambulation. The energy from this is from the Altar, for this is where the power comes from (within the Circumambulation). The throne and Dais of the Hierophant and other seated officers are limited here. Their power has already charged the temple and activated the Altar. The whole concept is an example of the current of Horus working with that of Osiris.

The Grip

1. The steps are taken and the Grip is exchanged simultaneously. Together, this means seeking guidance in the Darkness and silence of the Mysteries.

2. It shows that a steady and resolute will, acting in union with good, will accomplish what it desires no matter how often it fails at first. It inculcates the necessity for harmony and brotherly love—of doing away with pettiness and too much self concentration—for allowances for the weaknesses of others within limits—of shunning resolutely anything in the nature of slander. So that, in the Grip of the Neophyte, the Initiates meet hand to hand and foot to foot in the true greeting of brother and sister, and not in the veiled hostility of an enemy. For, in the working of the Inner, where all invoke the same forces in the same manner, if he becomes unsympathetic with the rest and so separates himself from them, though he weakens the combination of working, yet he still more certainly attracts upon himself a reflex current from the Avengers of Evil.

The name of Silence, which is the Grand Word of this Grade, also represents the Silence of the Sacred Mysteries to be observed toward the Outer Order. It shows also the necessity for respect towards the secrets of any Frater or Soror committed to your care, not endeavoring to search them out for the purpose of curiosity, not repeating them when discovered, nor in any way referring to them as a means of causing humiliation, but to keep them as sacred trust and not to be deflected by them from acting justly and harmoniously together.

3. In any magical ceremony or other working, if more than one member is taking part, all present putting themselves into the form of the god as taught should exchange Sign, Grip, and Words, so as to establish a current of harmony and the affirmation of a mutual direction of will toward the same object.

The Password

1. The password merely guards the Secrets of the Order against any members resigned or not working; hence it is changed each Equinox.

2. It is an affirmation of the different spiritual, as well as the different physical, constitutions of the Candidates—that all nature cannot be the same without evil and injury resulting thereby—but that each nature should be brought to its own Kether—the best of its kind. This, too, may be done in all things. It is the basis of Alchemy.

3. It should be pronounced as if attracting the solar force, the Light of Nature, during the six months following the Equinox at which it is issued, as a link with the solar force, between that and the Order. This password, therefore, may also be used in a magical ceremony as attracting the support of the Light of Nature acting upon natural forces.

After giving the words and signs, the Hiereus draws the Candidate forward between the Pillars and, for the second time in the Ceremony, the Higher Soul stands near and ready to touch the Candidate. The Hiereus returns to his place East of the Black Pillar so that the three chief officers may formulate and draw down to the Candidate, by their insignia and other influence of their symbols, the forces of the Supernal Triad. It is important, therefore, that, at this point, they should be in these places.

The Candidate now stands between the Pillars, bound with a rope like the mummified form of Osiris between Isis and Nepthys. The final consecration now takes place by the Goddess of the Scales of the Balance. The Candidate now stands, for the first time during the ceremony, at the point representing the equilibrium of balance. Meanwhile, the Kerux goes to the North, ready for the Circumambulation, so as to link that with the final consecration of the Candidate.

The final consecration is also demanded by the Hiereus—Horus the powerful Avenger of Osiris, as still menacing the Evil Persona of the Candidate. Its effect is to seal finally, in balanced formation, the four Pillars in the Sphere of Sensation of the Candidate. This does not imply that they were not naturally there before, but, in the natural human being, the symbols are unbalanced in strength—some weaker and some stronger. The effect of the ceremony is to strengthen the weak, purify the strong, and so begin to equilibrate them, and at the same time make a link between them and the corresponding forces of the Macrocosm.

The Effect of the Ceremony on the Sphere of Sensation

Previously, we have briefly touched upon the subject when dealing with the removal of the implements from the Altar and the Admission of the Candidate. The four Pillars thus referred to must at this point be distinguished from the Middle Pillar of the Candidate—which relates to the subtle body centers in the front of the body (which, for the purposes of a simple explanation, could be described as groups of minor chakras which have been grouped Kaballistically), not to be confused with the major

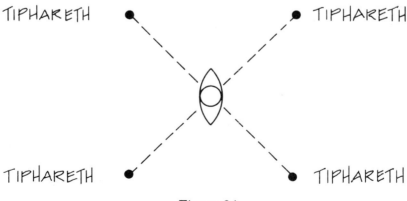

Figure 64
The Four Tiphareth Points

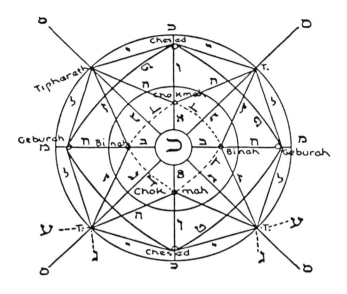

Figure 65
The Tree of Life in the Sphere of Sensation

chakras which are along the spine. The four Pillars represent the Aura of the Candidate. Taylor always taught us that this is what is most affected (the exception is the throat chakra at the back of the neck, which is touched directly by the sword of the Hiereus during the Obligation).

The Golden Dawn, according to Taylor, in its "word of mouth" teachings, considered that the body had seven basic auras and that each grade stimulated an aura. The Neophyte grade affects mainly the physical aura, which is also called the etheric double. It also must be remembered, though, that various parts of the soul which are considered distinct from the auras are also affected.

The Hierophant then commands the removal of the rope, which hitherto has been purposely retained. Symbolically, the rope restrains the actions of the natural human, whose temptations are toward the Evil Persona.

The four Pillars being thus firmly established, the Candidate is invested with the badge of the White Triangle of the Three Supernals formulating in Darkness. The Higher Self is enabled in reality to also consent. The free will of the natural human is never obsessed, either by the Higher Soul or by the ceremony, but, the will consenting, the whole of the ceremony is directed toward strengthening its actions. As the badge is placed upon him, it is as if the two Great Goddesses, Isis and Nepthys, stretch forth their wings over Osiris to restore him to life again.

The badge referred to is not a physical badge, but a symbolically placed symbol in the aura of the Candidate, on his forehead.

The Final Circumambulation in the Path of Light

The Mystic Circumambulation follows in the Path of Light to represent the rising Light in the Candidate, through the operation of self-sacrifice. As he passes the Hierophant's throne, the red Calvary Cross is astrally formed above the astral white triangle on his forehead, so that, so long as he belongs to the Order, he may bear the potent and sublime symbol as a link with his Higher Self and as an aid in searching out the forces of the Divine Light—if he will.

The Replacement of the Implements on the Altar

The manner of replacing these is the opposite to the figures above, which show how they were taken off the Altar. These represent the component parts of the Candidate, which have now been purified, and his Sphere of Sensation, which has now been equilibrated.

The Address to the Candidate

The Higher Soul or Genius now returns to the Invisible Station of Harpocrates, the place of the Hidden Center, while continuing to retain the link formed with the Candidate. The Address of the Hierophant is intended simply to effect the distinct formulation of the symbols of the 0=0 Grade of Neophyte in the Candidate, and it is therefore only when this is finished that the Watcher Anubis announces that the Candidate has been duly admitted as the initiated Neophyte. The Hiereus is charged with a warning address, as again confirming the will of the Candidate and addressing the final menace to the Evil Persona. The Hierophant states clearly that the symbols must be equilibrated in the Sphere of Sensation before a link can be formulated between them and the forces of the macrocosm. The necessity of examination is insisted upon so that this may be completely done.

Mixing of the Fluids

The Kerux pours out the two fluids to make the semblance of blood. This is to fix in the Candidate's sphere the symbols of the forces of transmutation in nature, and also to make an astral link between these and the Candidate's physical life, as a guard of the secrecy of the Mysteries. This particular form of transmutation is used as showing the effect of a mixture of forcing in producing a third appearance totally different from them. The red color is symbolic of the blood of the Candidate.

In the ancient Mysteries, the Candidate's blood was actually drawn at this time and preserved as an avenging link in case of his proving unworthy (consider the modern theory of Radionics and its effect on a blood sample). Transmutation effects matter quite well, seeing that the astral link is formally established.

The final speech of the Hierophant is further intended, beside its apparent meaning, to affirm that a person only partially initiated is neither fitted to teach nor to instruct even the outer and more ignorant in Sublime Knowledge. He is certain, through misunderstanding the principles, to formulate error instead of truth.

Closing of the Neophyte Grade

With the knock of the Hierophant, the generating current he created to keep the Light through the Portal starts to close. The cry of "Hekas, Hekas, Este Bebeloi" announces to all forces present in the Portal to leave. The four knocks of the officers then withdraw the Light, which then withdraws through the Hierophant—the second stage of the withdrawal. At this point, the Kerux must be ever watchful for any elemental force created during the ceremony, which might linger. There have been a number of instances in the past where there has been this type of residue left, which, if noticed, should be immediately banished by the Hiereus with the sword. The purification ceremony makes doubly sure that no negative side effects remain within the Hall.

Reverse Circumambulation

The reverse Circumambulation is intended to formulate the withdrawal of the Light of the Supernal Triad from the Altar so that it may not be profaned by abiding without due guard. Not that the Divine Light would suffer thereby, but because it might initiate an Avenging Current if profaned. This is what is implied by the Law of Moses in the prohibition about offering unconsecrated Fire either before or within the Veil of the Tabernacle. As a vibratory formula, the reverse Circumambulation represents the reversal of the current and the restoration of the operator to the ordinary condition. The mystic reverse Circumambulation forms its procession in the South, beginning from the Station of Dadouchos, as symbolic of the Ending Judgment of the World by Fire.

Partaking of the Eucharist

The Mystic Repast is communion in the body of Osiris. Its Mystic Name is "The Formula of the Justified One." The important point to remember is that, through the process of the ceremony, both the Paten and the Wine and Salt are magically transmuted through the magnetic influence of the ritual itself. This is done through the Osirian concept which is directed by the Hierophant. The Kerux, in finishing, inverts the Cup, as the Watcher of the God, to show that the symbols of self-sacrifice and of regeneration are accomplished. The proclamation is confirmed by the Hierophant, and the chief officers give three strokes, emblematic of the Mystic Triad, and repeat the Mystic Words. The Hierophant, in his final speech, seals the link, first formulated between the members of the Supernal Triad for each one present, that it may prove to him or her a guide for the ultimate attainment of the supreme initiation—if he will.

From Whare Ra Temple

Lecture on 0=0 Grade*

As I told you before, the 0=0 ceremony is one of the most important of our Order. You will see, I think, the reason for that in a moment, if you consider what it is that we are associated for. For we are here, a group drawn together from all conditions. If you take the whole Order, including the English, French, and Eastern Temples, it is still more noticeably the case. People of every grade of society, of every grade of opinion upon politics, religion, upon all subjects whereon people differ most, people who, if they were not members of this Order, would probably be flying at each other's throats, meet in perfect harmony and absolute trust, because they are all in search of the same thing. They approach it, however, from all sorts of different points. Men of science hope to find the realities which lie behind their subtlest investigations. Politicians, men and women who are anxious in some way or other to benefit humanity, hope that they will learn the secrets and reasons of some of the misfortunes which beset humanity, and how these misfortunes may be lifted. Physicians, hope that they may find the key to some of the deepest mysteries of human life, and human suffering, diseases, and death. And so,

---

*I am unaware of who wrote this lecture, but it was probably Mrs. R. W. Felkin.

187

from every point of view, men and women are drawn into the Order, in the hope that they may find the key to some of the mysteries which puzzle them most. And every one of them finds something which is to a certain degree repugnant. Some who come to us are trained with a contempt, it may be, or a distant distrust at any rate, for all ceremony, symbol, and ritual observance. Others come with a great liking for these things. Others, again, come with a great distaste for the learning of symbols, Hebrew letters, and the apparently meaningless objects of Archaic study. Some come with a great delight in all Archaic and mystic study. But within this Order all are treated exactly alike and in the same manner. If he or she wishes to progress, he or she must attend the ceremonies, must understand the ceremonies, the ritual, the symbology. All must learn the lectures and the archaic knowledge. All must go through the discipline, because that very point which to each is repugnant shows the point where he or she is out of key with the Brotherhood; shows an angle which must necessarily be rubbed off before he or she can be at all fitted for the building of the Temple.

Now, the ceremonies you are, as it were, shown and put through in actual physical practice and in the visible form are the Path, and the ceremonies which you will have to go through mentally, psychically, and spiritually in your future training and in your future occult life. And therefore the most important is the first entry into it.

The ritual of the 0=0 is, as I have said, full of symbology, and the symbology is that of the first emergence of the soul and the consciousness from the material, and its entry into the widest spiritual perception. It is somewhat in this way: as though a teacher beginning to train a class upon a vast subject should, partly by showing them a diagram upon a blackboard, it may be, or on a sheet of paper, of the whole course of study that they were to pass through, mapping out the line for them. Now this, in such a subject as ours, cannot wholly be done by diagram. There is so much of change, of growth, of progress, that has to be indicated, that it would take an infinite number of diagrams on paper to indicate what we can show by our ritual and ceremony within an hour. And every point in that ritual and ceremony has its correspondence in the future mental development of the Neophyte. And therefore every point should be carefully considered, since by it the Neophyte may know whether he or she is on the right line or not in his or her future progress. It would be impossible for me to tell you now the whole of the symbology and the mysteries contained in the ceremony of the 0=0 grade; because, even when you get into the Second Order, and when you attain to the rank of Minor Adeptship even, you have to wait for a considerable time before the full mysteries of the 0=0 ceremony and its full symbology are explained to you. Even if I were allowed to expound it more fully now, the words would be to all of you idle echoes. They would convey no meaning. But a certain amount I can tell you and a certain amount you can understand, and that amount will be quite enough to give you a great deal to think about.

Consider then, when you first enter the Temple in the 0=0 grade. You are, as a Neophyte, blindfolded, but after the hoodwinks are removed, you see. Now consider, what is the arrangement of the Temple when you come into it? The first thing that will strike you is the Altar in the center. That Altar signifies the Universe. The first thing that you have to learn is—that upon first entering occultism your minds must realize that there is a great deal beyond the material universe. By the material universe, I mean the entire universe, not only as far as the eye can reach, to the farthest star, but as far as you can conceive. The whole of that is symbolized by the cubical Altar, the double cube, which stands in the center of the room. Such must be the place that the material universe must occupy in your thoughts as you are thinking upon the subject of occultism. Hitherto it has bulked supreme in your minds, probably. Why a double cube, I shall come to later. But you know that the universe is subject to fixed laws. As far as ever you can trace by science or by induction, the universe is subject to fixed laws, some of which you can formulate, and from that formulation you can deduce others, showing that in all your science and all your undertakings you postulate fixed laws. Now these fixed laws are outside and beyond the universe, therefore upon the universe as operated on by fixed laws do you fix your thoughts. Now you see upon either side of the Altar two seats, occupied by Stolistes in the North and Dadouchos in the South, Stolistes bearing the Cup and Dadouchos the Censer. These are the powers of Water and Fire, the powers of cold and heat, the receptive and the energizing, the negative and the positive, the female and the male. And between them lies the universe. That is the first lesson that you have to learn.

Then you see at the East the throne of the Hierophant, and at the West the throne of the Hiereus. The Hiereus is in a black robe and bearing a sword. The Hierophant is in a red robe and bearing a crown-headed scepter. This symbolizes the powers of Light and Darkness. Again we see the conception of the positive and energizing and the negative or receptive. Darkness absorbs all things. Light manifests and reveals all things. Between the darkness and the light vibrates the Veil of Colors of the Earth. These again are operating upon the cubical Altar, and so you have, as it were, four strenuous streams of force directed upon the universe; and that is the first thought that must occupy the mind of the student just emerging from the outside world, from the condition of material darkness, into the study of occultism. Not only that; from his study of the universe he finds certain laws prevailing,[1] and therefore assumes that these laws operate more and more widely still, reasoning from the smaller to the greater. He must take, as it were, the Sight of the Eye of GOD, and see the universe as a small speck operated upon by the four powers, who present themselves to the thought of the student as four Angels, or as four Gods according to the earlier system. The Angels of the Egyptian, Gnostic, and Christian systems are all personifications of the Four Forces operating upon the universe, which you see personified by the principle officers in the Hall of the Neophyte—Raphael, Gabriel, Michael, Auriel. Then, just beyond

---

[1]Throughout this chapter, the masculine pronoun is used in its generic sense to indicate either sex.

the Altar, you see two Pillars. These two Pillars represent the same idea in another form; they are the Pillars of Light and of Darkness, the Pillars of Fire and of Cloud of the Israelites wandering in the wilderness. They are the Pillars of Jachin and Boaz of the Temple of Solomon. And between them is another chief officer, the Hegemon, with the white robe and the miter-headed scepter; the white robe also signifying the synthesis of all color. I told you that between the blinding Light and the absolute Darkness vibrates the Veil of Color, and the synthesis, the combination, of all colors is white. The robe of the Hierophant is flame red because the blinding light which issues from the radiant East is that which no eye of man can gaze upon unharmed, and therefore a symbolic color is chosen. Now, fixing the attention for a moment upon the Hegemon, you see that the Hegemon represents the synthesis and the equilibrium of all the forces that act upon the universe. Therefore the Hegemon sits between the two Pillars, representing the perfect equilibrium; between them is the universe. And carrying the thought beyond the universe to the point of equilibrium you see the two Pillars forming as it were a gateway. Between them the Hegemon who is to receive the student of occultism. Such then must be the mental pose of the student, once the student sees the diagram, once the student is taken through it at his initiation. And the intention is that ever afterwards that ceremony and the plan of the whole shall dwell upon his mind and be always present to his mind, in order that he may attain the proper pose of mind to pass on to learn the secret of the universe. At the very opening of the next grade, passing from 0=0 of Neophyte to the 1=10, the first words the Neophyte hears are: "Prepare to enter the immeasurable regions." Now remember, the cubical Altar is the measurable. You desire to learn the secret and the meanings of the forces that operate upon the universe, therefore you must first enter the immeasurable regions. You will never learn them as long as you are within bounds and measures. But mentally elevate the thought above and beyond the region which is measurable, and you will begin to see the forces which form infinity act upon the finite universe. Now, let's go a little more into particulars. This

Altar is a double cube; i.e., it has ten squares which are visible if you walk around it and examine it all over. But, if you are standing upon the Earth and looking at the universe, as a man of science stands upon the Earth and contemplates the universe, as the materialist of any sort contemplates the universe, the cubical Altar is, as it were, raised immediately above the head, so that he can only see the bottom square upon which it stands. Hidden from him by the bottom square are nine other squares. Now the bottom square of the cubical Altar represents all that possibly can be learned by logic and deduction, or by the five senses, by any scientific instrument, by any scientific discovery. A minute and perfect acquaintance with the bottom square of the cubical Altar is the whole that can be gained. Therefore the Neophyte has first of all to learn to put things in their proper place. In this Order no scientific attainment and no scientific discovery is despised or undervalued. On the contrary, it is most highly valued and most highly esteemed. The Neophyte, however, desiring to enter the path of Occult Science, has to remember that the whole of the universe is represented by the cubical Altar in the center, and that the whole of scientific investigation is represented by one tenth of that cubical Altar. And note also that the Altar stands upon its bottom square. The bottom square is therefore out of sight in the ceremonies of the Order. Why? Not because we undervalue the bottom square. On the contrary, we recognize that it is the foundation. It is the basis upon which our Altar stands. But in the studies and in the ceremonies of this Order, it is other things which we investigate and consider. Our Altar must have its basis and we must stand firm upon that basis. This is the position, not only of science, but of everything that can be attained by discovery, by the five senses of the logical brain.

Now, the same ideas are resumed in the implements and the ornaments that lie upon the Altar. At the East end of the Altar there lie one or two roses. At the North end is the Paten with bread and salt. At the South end is the Lamp of Fire. At the West end is the Cup. There is also the Colored Cross and the White Triangle.

According to our teaching, and according to the idea which I want every student to grasp, and to hold in his hand, these resume the ideas, showing how the forces, operating from the four Angels from outside the universe, are reflected in the universe itself. And therefore we can trace the operations of these Angels who are outside of the phenomena which we can observe in the material universe. Now, when the Neophyte is brought into the Hall, all these things are arranged round him, but he sees them not. He is brought in blindfolded and with a rope round his waist, and this is also the mental condition in which the Neophyte must continue his occult study. He must not imagine that he will mentally see what it all means. Not until he has been inside for some time, will he see. Immediately he begins the Path of Occult Study he will be aware of things of which he knows the meaning, certain strange thoughts, strange ideas, and strange questionings as to whether there may not be something or other discoverable behind the veil of matter, which hitherto he has regarded as impenetrable, but they will be but vague voices, vague sounds, vague hints, just as when he comes blindfolded into the Temple he hears vague sounds, vague voices, perhaps some of them familiar voices, some of them not, moving of feet, and so on. He is led on a path he knows not. But why does he go forward? Because he has a certain amount of faith. Because he believes that somehow or another something will be shown to him bye and bye, and that the hoodwink will be taken from his eyes. Now he must learn that in order not to be impatient, because at the beginning of occult study he is unable to see what it all means, or unable to see what any of it means, whither it is tending. Mentally he is hoodwinked, mentally he is bound by the finite conditions out of which he has just emerged. And therefore, his mental pose must be to not be impatient with the blindfolding and with the rope and with the conditions of finite limitations which he is still under, but to believe that he is under the charge of someone who knows, and bye and bye those limitations will be removed. Now in the full Temple ceremony there is a Sentinel outside the door armed with a sword. Practically in most of our ceremonies the Sentinel is dispensed with, but the Sentinel nevertheless has an important symbology. Because, you will notice, one of the chief officers goes outside the Temple to bring in the Neophyte. Such an officer is known to the Sentinel, and the Sentinel allows the Neophyte, blindfolded, to pass in, in company of the initiate who is known to him. Otherwise the Sentinel is armed with a lethal weapon to strike any intruder who is rash enough to attempt to enter the Portals. Now that is an absolutely true symbology of those who attempt, themselves, without initiation, to force a way into the Occult Mysteries. It is a well-known fact, which I think every physician will testify to, that all who have tried to do so have either failed miserably, being driven back by the Sentinel, or have paid the penalty in the madhouse or in the grave. The initiation comes from within. The message is sent from within to bring the Neophyte into the Temple where he may be taught. The Sentinel's weapon is lowered and he is allowed to pass. Translating that into the material language of everyday life, everyone knows the miserable end to which would-be mediums or students of spiritualist phenomena come usually, if they attain any amount of psychic development without proper training. Whereas, in our Order, everyone has before him the example of others who have trodden the same path, and who are to testify, not only with their voices, but to show by example that the path is safe. But for all of you, as it happens, I stand the most advanced among you, as the only one who has passed into the Second Order, and I can assure you therefore both by my word and by my example that the path is absolutely safe both to brain and body. And to me where I stand there are others far in advance of me who are able to give me the same assurance of the perfect safety of the path, and who are able to instruct me, as I am able to instruct you, on every step of the road. So the Neophyte is brought past the Sentinel, whose weapon is so deadly to those who strive to force their way in.

Then within the doors stands the Kerux, carrying the wand and the lamp. Immediately the student enters mentally the Path of Occult Wisdom, there is a lamp which always goes before him. But at first he sees it not, at first he appears to himself to be wandering in darkness. I want really to emphasize this point strongly, because it is the experience of every student who enters the Path of Occult Knowledge. In the first steps he appears to be wandering in darkness, and he appears to be going he knows not whither and by a devious road and without a guide. It is for that reason he is led in various circumambulations which all have their meaning, but whose meaning is carefully concealed from the Neophyte. His mental attitude is precisely the same, and must remain the same for some time to come. Now the Kerux leads him on the path round and about the Temple, but observe, not to the point of equilibrium for a long time. First of all he has to show his earnestness by pledging himself to the duties of the Order he is about to join, and to the diligent prosecution of Occult Science, to secrecy and to the Brotherhood. And this pledge is an absolute translation into words of the mental character he has to cultivate. Observe therefore that your mental pose must be that which you take up as a Neophyte in the Hall of the Neophytes in the Temple. The Neophyte is helped at various points by various officers. For example, the Hiereus threatens him with the Sword of Darkness, and the Hierophant menaces him with the Scepter of Light. He has to know both extremes before he can know the equilibrium, again an absolute picture of the mental state. This state must vibrate, it must touch the extreme of darkness and it must face the blinding light, but being able to bear neither, it finds that there is no rest in either before it can reach the point of equilibrium. And moreover he must undergo the purification by fire and the purification by water, he must be consecrated by the Stolistes and the Dadouchos. He must, that is, be purged of the influence both of the negative and of the positive, that the limitations and the evil beginnings to those two qualities may be rooted from his mind, and that his mind may attain an absolute equipoise. Thrice must this mystic consecration be repeated, and at last he may be deemed to be purified from the limitations and the evils relating to those two qualities of water and fire. Then at last he is brought up between the Mystical Pillar, into the symbolic gateway of Occult Science. Then the Hierophant advances from his throne to meet him and draws him between the Pillars, thus acknowledging that he has attained the equilibrium. Now that is the condition of mind that the student has first to attain to, coming in from wandering in darkness, by his faith, passing round under the influence of all the four Angels who operate upon the universe and whose operations produce all the phenomena we know and see. At last faith changes to sight. He is brought up to and attains equilibrium of mind. That is only the first step, and it is a step which will probably take the student a long time to attain. Therefore let the student examine his own mental state and mental pose from time to time, and try to see whereabouts he is mentally in the Initiation Ceremony.

The Lamp of the Kerux will always go before him. Let him then understand that the Light is before him though he sees it not. He will see it bye and bye, and therefore let him understand that the mind, being set right, and earnestly desiring truth, and earnestly desiring absolute goodness, it is impossible for him to go wrong. Any step he takes is guided, though he knows it not. And if it be any help or any consolation to those who still find it difficult to realize this, I may say of my own knowledge that a time arrives when, a certain advancement having been made, it is possible to see. To every one of you this is possible. Only advance far enough and the hoodwink will be removed off your eyes, and you will actually see and know the Divine Guidance of the Kerux of the universe guiding the step of every Neophyte. The Neophyte is hoodwinked and knows it not, but you will know it and you will see it, though you may not at the moment be able to tell him. Those of us who have advanced far enough can say of our own knowledge that for every student who is really striving in earnest for the Occult Science it is really absolute fact that the Lamp of the Kerux goes before him and not one single wrong step can be taken. Then you notice that as you go on to different ceremonies of the Order that these Pillars are in different parts of the Hall, signifying for you your progress in the Order. The gateway of Occult Science is behind you in some senses, before you in others. It is in one direction or another direction according to your progress. Standing firm upon its fourfold basis is the black square, symbolic of the materiality upon which we all stand, but bearing upon its summit the triangle symbolic of water and the triangle symbolic of fire. The two triangles and the lamp signifying the Divine Essence on the summit. Observe now there is the seat of the Stolistes, there is the triangle of fire, there is the platter of salt signifying the Earth. You are therefore not to conclude that all materiality comes from one direction, or all the spirituality from one direction. In every direction in the Hall you will find, if you study the symbols, that all the elements are united, but some are more prominent according as you fix your attention on one point or another. The position of the Great Angels ruling the universe does not cause them to throw their influence solely and immediately upon that point of the universe that is opposite to their feet, for that would produce discord and want of equilibrium at once; and the influence of the elements again are counterchanged and not even in such regularity and absolute symmetry as could be explained now, but according to a very complex method of counterchanging, the effect of which is to produce that equilibrium which is the keynote of the teaching of the grade.

Now further you are to understand that the signs of the grade are to be very carefully given. The signs of the grade are not conventional forms, not merely signs of groping, although that is their first meaning. This is the sign also of the giving out of force. It is the sign of entering the Portal, and further a sign of humility, and the bowing of the head to a greater light and a greater power. To give the signs properly, you should always remember to give the step of the left foot, which should be given firmly, and the hands should be raised above the head and lowered to the level of the eyes and the hands should be pointed straight. The vital force emanates from the eyes and the hands, and these should be all in the same line, with the foot firmly planted on the ground. That sign is not merely a sign of groping or of respect in passing the throne of the Hierophant, but it is an occult sign of great power whose meaning you will learn hereafter when you enter upon the study of practical magic.

Now, one thing more with regard to this grade. You are to remember that the Hall of the Neophyte, and in fact the whole Temple of the Order of the S.·.M.·. represents as it were the

porch of the Temple. When your feet are well planted in the
porch, you are well on your way to entering the Temple. You must
therefore look upon it as though, at this end of the Temple, and
behind the throne of the Hierophant, there was a veil extended
separating the Outer from the Inner, and that through the veil,
as a priest emerging from the Temple, comes the Hierophant to
instruct, to initiate, to perform ceremonies which are really of
magical import. So, in the same way, you should not look upon
any other Adepti who are present. You in the Order can know
nothing about these or their grade, you merely know that they
are members of the Second Order and that they have attained the
grade of 5=6. They may be Minor, Major, or still higher, but,
passed within the veil, they are lost to your sight. They come
forth in the Temple ceremonies as veiled figures whose advancement in the Outer you can know nothing of. That is the way
mentally in which you should look at your own mental future.
Now when you have passed through the 0=0 grade, you have a
certain lecture, the first knowledge lecture, to study, and no
doubt all of you who have had that first knowledge lecture will
consider it rather a heterogeneous mass of archaic knowledge of
various kinds, none of which matters much, and most of which
you were familiar with before. But there is really a good deal
more in it than this. Of course anyone who has studied mystic
subjects at all is probably familiar with such things as the
symbols of the signs of the Zodiac, the Planets, and the Hebrew
letters. But these symbols are not chosen by chance, but because
they are absolutely necessary to further advance. And I may
mention here that it is especially desired by the Greatly Honored
Chiefs who guide us in the Second Order that all students should
be most exactly particular in the drawing of the symbols and in
the form of the Hebrew letters. Of course there is a current
Hebrew which some of us may write and which is often badly
written. That has nothing more to do with it than writing an
English word. But everyone should know the exact form of each
symbol and each letter, and be able on occasion to draw them
clearly, beautifully, and with mathematical accuracy, because
these symbols are not merely conventional symbols. Every one

has a meaning. If you will take for instance the symbol of Fire (△) and the symbol of Water (▽), these are as I have told you the symbols of the Great Gods, and particularly appropriate symbols because the aspiring of the Fire always tending upwards is well shown by the triangle pointed upwards, while the instability, but perfectly horizonal surface, of Water is well shown by the triangle pointed down. And the bar across (△) and the bar across (▽) give us the Hexagram, the equilibrium of the elements, the atonement, and therefore give you these elements as they are in the universe. Hence Earth and Air are the more material and physical representations of the same forces as Fire and Water. And that is the meaning of the bar across which converts Water into Earth and Fire into Air. Then take the ordinary symbol of Aries (♈); perhaps you will say it is a very ordinary symbol of a goat's head and horns. So it is. Now what was the symbology of "animal" according to the Egyptian and according to the Qabbalistic schemes? "Animal" signified the lower part of man's nature which was to be sacrificed. What then does the ram signify? Sensuality by all the schemes. Now this signifies also the Pentagram, but the evil Pentagram, the Goat of Mendes. How then should the Ram or Lamb be the divine symbol? The symbol of the Vernal Equinox? The symbol of the Dawning Light? Because the ram must be slain, the ram's head inverted; the evil passions subdued and sacrificed, the sensuality cast out. The lamb which was slain, the symbol of the dawning light of the universe, the symbol of the Golden Dawn. As you see, there is a great deal in that symbol of Aries (♈) read properly. And so again the symbol of Taurus (♉) the bull; the symbol of Earth unites for us the two great lights: the greater light that rules the day and the lesser light that rules the night. These symbolize for us the light and the darkness, yet both illuminated by the divine rays, and therefore the equilibrium, which is the key of progress upon the Earth plane. And so we might go through every symbol of the signs of the Zodiac if there were time. We might deduce a great many lessons from them, but the one lesson that I want to emphasize now is that above all, the symbols must be accurately learned.

I think I told many of you before now that the planetary symbols are formed from the circle, the crescent, and the cross; the cross signifying corrosion, the circle signifying the red, and the crescent the white metals, giving you thus the metals of every planet, and giving you, when you get far enough to understand it, the meaning and influence of every planet. Giving you also, when you get further on still, a key to color, a key to the symbology of that veil of color which vibrates between the light and the darkness. It is not for nothing that the iron, whose color is greenish, in its corrosion becomes red, and that copper whose color is red in its corrosion becomes green. All these have a symbology. Every planet has its color; every sign of the Zodiac has its color; every element has its color. Every symbol in the world has its appropriate color, and every color in the world has its meaning. And the meanings rightly interpreted give the key to much of the physical and material science which is absolutely dark at present because the meaning and the color are not known.

Now, the grouping of the planets, and of the signs of the Zodiac, according to their triplicities, and according to the signs they govern, is extremely important because it gives one the key to the influences which are most strongly directed upon this part of the universe from those Four Great Angels from whom we have seen those forces operating upon the material universe, where they are concentrated and summed up. The ring of the Zodiac is around the world, and the world turns round and presents a different face to each sign in turn. And from the different directions of that wheel are various forces constantly flowing in upon the world. Not in exact equilibrium, for exact equilibrium for the world would mean the cessation of life. The present material and finite life of the world depends upon a certain want of equilibrium. The progress of the student out of the finite into the Infinite Knowledge depends upon his knowledge of the forces flowing in upon the world, which indeed are all equal and in exact harmony, but which, not all falling at the same precise moment of time, are slightly out of equilibrium at each particular point, and therefore by that slight want of equilibrium producing slight transient change. Therefore the influence and connection of elements, planets, and signs is to be so carefully studied that it becomes absolutely a component part of oneself, and then when the correspondences are learned further on the mental, psychical, and spiritual, results will be immediately perceived. Now, finally in the first knowledge lecture you get the study of the Hebrew alphabet, and the formation of the Hebrew letters is most essential. I can only give you a very slight idea of one or two small points indicating where the great importance comes in. If you take the Hebrew alphabet to be formed from the *Yod* (׳), that is the first beginnings, the first thought of the alphabet. And if you look at it I think that it will remind you above all of a tongue of flame curling up from a fire, an escaped tongue of fire not burning centrally as a lamp or candle, but flying off without any material to feed its flame. There are many other symbolisms connected with this *Yod,* many much deeper, but that will do for the present because it will give you the root idea of the *Yod* in easy, simple form. Now, the *Yod* (׳) brought down to Earth plane (the *Yod* lies above the line in writing) as a fire burning upon the Earth, or a fire influencing the Earth, becomes the letter *Vau* (ו). Here then we have two letters of the Great Fourfold Name of God (ה ו ה י) and two of them indicate the Fire. Now we pass from *Yod* to the first letter of the Hebrew alphabet, *Aleph* (א). This consists of three *Yods*—an elongated one very much like *Vau* between two others, and there you have the Three in One: the Three Fire Spirits, the Three Energizing Spirits from whom proceeded all things; i.e., the Great Unity.

Now the next letter, *Beth* (ב), is the Binary, the Two. If I put a *Beth* beside an archaic ב , you will see that they are very near each other in shape, so near that it is tolerably certain that one was drawn from the other. The Binary is the great point which we have been considering so far, the two forces, the positive and the negative, the Severity and the Mercy which are united in the equilibrium. Therefore AB or ABBA represents the Father. Another symbology in the Binary is that it is almost identically the figure of a swan sailing over the water, the swan being symbolic of the elements of Air and Water, as the *Aleph* (א) is symbolic of the three *Yods* of Fire, Air, and Water, therefore the elements that are the cause of Earth are the three that are synthesized in Earth. Also, *Beth* (ב) is a house, and is the representation of a lean-to shed against a wall on a section. I give you this to show that the forms of the Hebrew letters are of very great importance. Then *Gimel* (ג) is the third letter, the letter of production or emergence. A plane, an emergence or passing through, that was the glyph of Horus, a glyph of birth also. Now in the Qabbalistic scheme there was no feminine represented among the causes of the universe. The first great Causa Causans was the Father-Mother, but Isis was Nature. Osiris was male-female, therefore the Spirit, which according to some schemes was not as mystic as the Hebrew, was feminine, is represented masculine by the addition of the *Yod*. Now therefore you have the first glyph of the:

    Aleph א Three in One

    Beth ב Two, the House

    Gimel ג Emergence, the Birth

And the three together representing the origin of the alphabet, the origin of the Word, the origin of things.

The *Daleth,* the square (ד) or this wise, ⊤ , the Mason's Square. Or you may put a cross in a diamond-shaped square (⊕) then you need only one line to represent a square. You have your cross which signifies the world and an indication of the quaternary or square beyond it ( )+). So the ד and the 4 are the same symbol.

I do not propose to go any further with the Hebrew alphabet. I just indicated that to show you the enormous importance of being absolutely accurate with the forms. And remember, above all things when making your Hebrew letters to make them square. Avoid all cursiveness, that is, in writing anything for inscription or mystic working of any kind. You will not yet be able to use the Hebrew letters for magical ceremonies or anything of that kind, but hereafter you will, and you will find that, if you have got a careless style in writing Hebrew, and you do not fully understand the exact shape of every letter (and I talk as one who has tried and knows), that you will fail in your ceremony and you will fail absolutely as if you made a chemical combination with false weights or as if you had painted a picture with dirty muddy colors. Absolute accuracy is the only road to success. Every letter must be drawn with as perfect form and perfect intention as if you were making a mathematical working drawing for an engineer to make a machine from. Get out of your head the notion that you are writing a current language when you are making mystic words and symbols.

STAY IN TOUCH

On the following pages you will find listed, with their current prices, some of the books and tapes now available on related subjects. Your book dealer stocks most of these, and will stock new titles in the Llewellyn series as they become available. We urge your patronage.

However, to obtain our full catalog, to keep informed of new titles as they are released and to benefit from informative articles and helpful news, you are invited to write for our bi-monthly news magazine/catalog. A sample copy is free, and it will continue coming to you at no cost as long as you are an active mail customer. Or you may keep it coming for a full year with a donation of just $2.00 in U.S.A. ($7.00 for Canada & Mexico, $20.00 overseas, first class mail). Many bookstores also have *The Llewellyn New Times* available to their customers. Ask for it.

Stay in touch! In *The Llewellyn New Times'* pages you will find news and reviews of new books, tapes and services, announcements of meetings and seminars, articles helpful to our readers, news of authors, advertising of products and services, special money-making opportunities, and much more.

The Llewellyn New Times
P.O. Box 64383-Dept. 897, St. Paul, MN 55164-0383, U.S.A.

•   •   •

TO ORDER BOOKS AND TAPES

If your book dealer does not have the books and tapes described on the following pages readily available, you may order them direct from the publisher by sending full price in U.S. funds, plus $2.00 for postage and handling for the first book, and 50¢ for each additional book. There are no postage and handling charges for orders over $50. UPS Delivery: We ship UPS whenever possible. Delivery guaranteed. Provide your street address as UPS does not deliver to P.O. Boxes. UPS to Canada requires a $50 minimum order. Allow 4-6 weeks for delivery. Orders outside the U.S.A. and Canada: Airmail—add retail price of book; add $5 for each non-book item (tapes, etc.); add $1 per item for surface mail.

FOR GROUP STUDY AND PURCHASE

Because there is a great deal of interest in group discussion and study of the subject matter of this book, we feel that we should encourage the adoption and use of this particular book by such groups by offering a special "quantity" price to group leaders or "agents."

Our Special Quantity Price for a minimum order of five copies of *Z-5: Secret Teachings of the Golden Dawn (Book 1: The Neophyte Ritual 0=0)* is $38.85 cash-with-order. This price includes postage and handling within the United States. Minnesota residents must add 6% sales tax. For additional quantities, please order in multiples of five. For Canadian and foreign orders, add postage and handling charges as above. Credit card (VISA, MC, Amex) orders are accepted. Charge card orders only may be phoned free ($15.00 minimum order) within the U.S.A. or Canada by dialing 1-800-THE MOON. Customer service calls dial 1-612-291-1970. Mail Orders to:

LLEWELLYN PUBLICATIONS
P.O. Box 64383-Dept. 897 / St. Paul, MN 55164-0383, U.S.A.

GOLDEN DAWN ENOCHIAN MAGIC
by Pat Zalewski
Enochian magic is considered by most magicians to be the most powerful system ever created. Aleister Crowley, "The Great Beast," learned this system of magic from the Hermetic Order of the Golden Dawn, which had developed and expanded the concepts and discoveries of Elizabethan magus John Dee. This book picks up where the published versions of the Enochian material of the Golden Dawn leave off.

Based on the research and unpublished papers of MacGregor Mathers, one of the founders of the Golden Dawn, *Golden Dawn Enocian Magic* opens new avenues of use for this system. New insights are given on such topics as the Sigillum Dei Aemeth, the Angels of the Enochian Aires applied to the 12 tribes of Israel and the Kabbalah, the 91 Governors, the Elemental Tablets as applied to the celestial sphere, and more. This book provides a long-sought break from amateurish and inaccurate books on the subject; it is designed to complement such scholarly classics as *Enochian Invocation* and *Heptarchia Mystica*.

0-87542-898-3, 224 pgs., 6 x 9, illus. $12.95

THE GOLDEN DAWN
by Israel Regardie
The Original Account of the Teachings, Rites and Ceremonies of the Hermetic Order of the Golden Dawn as revealed by Israel Regardie, with further revision, expansion, and additional notes by Regardie, Cris Monnastre, and others. Expanded with an index of more than 100 pages!

Originally published in four bulky volumes of some 1200 pages, this 6th Revised and Enlarged Edition has been entirely reset in modern, less space-consuming type, in half the pages (while retaining the original pagination in marginal notation for reference) for greater ease and use.

Corrections of typographical errors perpetuated in the original and subsequent editions have been made, with further revision and additional text and notes by noted scholars and by actual practitioners of the Golden Dawn system of Magick, with an Introduction by the only student ever accepted for personal training by Regardie.

Also included are Initiation Ceremonies, important rituals for consecration and invocation, methods of meditation and magical working based on the Enochian Tablets, studies in the Tarot, and the system of Qabalistic Correspondences that unite the World's religions and magical traditions into a comprehensive and practical whole.

This volume is designed as a study and practice curriculum suited to both group and private practice. Meditation upon, and following with the Active Imagination, the Initiation Ceremonies is fully experiential without need of participation in group or lodge. A very complete reference encyclopedia of Western Magick.

0-87542-663-8, 803 pages, 6 x 9, illus. $19.95

A GARDEN OF POMEGRANATES
by Israel Regardie
What is the Tree of Life? It's the ground plan of the Qabalistic system—a set of symbols used since ancient times to study the Universe. The Tree of Life is a geometrical arrangement of ten sephiroth, or spheres, each of which is associated with a different archetypal idea, and 22 paths which connect the spheres.

This system of primal correspondences has been found the most efficient plan ever devised to classify and organize the characteristics of the self. Israel Regardie has written one of the best and most lucid introductions to the Qabalah.

A Garden of Pomegranates combines Regardie's own studies with his notes on the works of Aleister Crowley, A.E. Waite, Eliphas Levi and D.H. Lawrence. No longer is the wisdom of the Qabalah to be held *secret!* The needs of today place the burden of growth upon each and every person—each has to undertake the Path as his or her own responsibility, but every help is given in the most ancient and yet most modern teaching here known to humankind.

0-87542-690-5, 176 pgs., softcover $6.95

THE MIDDLE PILLAR
by Israel Regardie
Between the two outer pillars of the Qabalistic Tree of Life, the extremes of Mercy and Severity, stands THE MIDDLE PILLAR, signifying one who has achieved equilibrium in his or her own self.

Integration of the human personality is vital to the continuance of creative life. Without it, man lives as an outsider to his own true self. By combining Magic and Psychology in the Middle Pillar Ritual/Exercise (a magical meditation technique), we bring into balance the opposing elements of the psyche while yet holding within their essence and allowing full expression of man's entire being.

In this book, and with this practice, you will learn to: understand the psyche through its correspondences on the Tree of Life; expand self-awareness, thereby intensifying the inner growth process; activate creative and intuitive potentials; understand the individual thought patterns which control every facet of personal behavior; regain the sense of balance and peace of mind—the equilibrium that everyone needs for physical and psychic health.

0-87542-658-1, 176 pgs., softcover $6.95

20th CENTURY MAGIC AND THE OLD RELIGION: DION FORTUNE, CHRISTINE HARTLEY, CHARLES SEYMOUR
by Alan Richardson

This magical record details the work of two senior magicians—Charles Seymour and Christine Hartley—within Dion Fortune's Society of the Inner Light during the years 1937 to 1939.

Using juxtaposed excerpts from Seymour and Hartley's magical diaries together with biographical prefaces containing unique insights into the background and nature of the Society, Alan Richardson paints a fascinating picture of Dion Fortune and her fellow adepts at the peak of their magical careers.

Originally published as *Dancers to the Gods*, now with a new introduction and the addition of Seymour's long essay, "The Old Religion," a manual of self-initiation, this new edition retains Dion Fortune's "lost" novels, the past-life identities of her Secret Chiefs, and much more.

The simple act of reading these juxtaposed diaries of a true priest and priestess can cause a resonance with the soul which will ultimately transform those who so desire it.

0-87542-673-5, 288 pgs., photographs, 6 x 9   **$12.95**

ANCIENT MAGICKS FOR A NEW AGE
by Alan Richardson and Geoff Hughes

With two sets of personal magickal diaries, this book details the work of magicians from two different eras. In it, you can learn what a particular magician is experiencing in this day and age, how to follow a similar path of your own, and discover correlations to the workings of traditional adepti from almost half a century ago.

The first set of diaries are from Christine Hartley and show the magick performed within the Merlin Temple of the Stella Matutina, an offshoot of the Hermetic Order of the Golden Dawn, in the years 1940-42. The second set are from Geoff Hughes, and detail his magickal work during 1984-86. Although he was not at that time a member of any formal group, the magick he practiced was under the same aegis as Hartley's. The third section of this book, written by Hughes, shows how you can become your own Priest or Priestess and make contact with Merlin.

The magick of Christine Hartley and Geoff Hughes are like the poles of some hidden battery that lies beneath the Earth and beneath the years. There is a current flowing between them, and the energy is there for you to tap.

0-87542-671-9, 320 pgs., illus., 6 X 9   **$12.95**

IMAGICK: THE MAGICK OF IMAGES, PATHS & DANCE
by Ted Andrews

The Qabala is rich in spiritual, mystical and magickal symbols. These symbols are like physical tools, and when you learn to use them correctly, you can construct a bridge to reach the energy of other planes. The secret lies in merging the outer world with inner energies, creating a flow that augments and enhances all aspects of life.

Imagick explains effective techniques of bridging the outer and inner worlds through visualization, gesture, and dance. It is a synthesis of yoga, sacred dance and Qabalistic magick that can enhance creativity, personal power, and mental and physical fitness.

This is one of the most personal magickal books ever published, one that goes far beyond the "canned" advice other books on Pathworking give you. You will learn how the energies reflected in such things as color vibration, names, letters, tarot associations and astrological relationships radiate from the "temple" of each sephiroth.
0-87542-016-8, 6 x 9, 312 pgs., illus. **$12.95**

SIMPLIFIED MAGIC
by Ted Andrews

In every person, the qualities essential for accelerating his or her growth and spiritual evolution are innate, but even those who recognize such potentials need an effective means of releasing them. The ancient and mystical Qabala is that means.

A person does not need to become a dedicated Qabalist in order to acquire benefits from the Qabala. *Simplified Magic* offers a simple understanding of what the Qabala is and how it operates. It provides practical methods and techniques so that the energies and forces within the system and within ourselves can be experienced in a manner that enhances growth and releases our greater potential. *A reader knowing absolutely nothing about the Qabala could apply the methods in this book with noticeable success!*

The Qabala is more than just some theory for ceremonial magicians. It is a system for personal attainment and magic that anyone can learn and put to use in his or her life. The secret is that the main glyph of the Qabala, the Tree of Life, is *within* you. The Tree of Life is a map to the levels of consciousness, power and magic that are within. By learning the Qabala you will be able to tap into these levels and bring peace, healing, power, love, light and magic into your life.
0-87542-015-X, 210 pgs., illus., softcover **$3.95**

MYSTERIA MAGICA
by Denning and Phillips

For years, Denning and Phillips headed the international occult Order Aurum Solis. In this book they present the magickal system of the order so that you can use it. Here you will find rituals for banishing and invoking plus instructions for proper posture and breathing. You will learn astral projection, rising on the planes, and the magickal works that should be undertaken through astral projection. You will learn the basic principle of ceremonies and how to make sigils and talismans. You will learn practical Enochian magick plus how to create, consecrate and use your magickal tools such as the magickal sword, wand and cup. You will also learn the advanced arts of sphere-working and evocation to visible appearance.

Filled with illustrations, this book is an expanded version of the previous edition. It is now complete in itself and can be the basis of an entire magickal system. You can use the information alone or as the sourcebook for a group. It is volume 3 of **The Magical Philosophy**, the other two books being *The Sword and The Serpent* and *The Foundations of High Magick*. If you want to learn how to do real magick, this is the place you should start.

0-87542-196-2, 480 pgs., 6 x 9, illus., softcover   **$15.00**

THE SWORD AND THE SERPENT: The Magical Structure
of Cosmos and Psyche
Being a revision and expansion of Books III and IV of the first edition.
by Denning and Phillips

This is the comprehensive guide to the Magical Qabalah with extensive correspondences as well as the techniques for activating the centers, use of images and the psychology of attainment.

In this volume, histories from contemporary life together with references to the works of mystics, poets, artists, philosophers and authorities in psychology are cited to illustrate point by point the action and interaction of the functions of the psyche as identified in Qabalistic teaching.

In this book is set forth clearly the real meaning of adepthood: in relation to this, frequent enigmas of occult literature such as the Abyss, the Knowledge and Conversation of the Holy Guardian Angel, and the supernal attainments, are presented in their true meaning and significance. The natural dignity and potential of life in this world is your birthright. In this volume, its splendor and power are made unmistakably manifest.

0-87542-197-0, 512 pgs., 6 x 9, illus., softcover   **$15.00**

PLANETARY MAGICK
by Denning & Phillips
This book is filled with guidelines and rites for powerful magical action. There are rites for the individual magician, rites for the magical group. The rites herein are given *in full*, and are revealed for the first time. Planetary Magick provides a full grasp of the root system of Western Magick, a system which evolved in Babylonia and became a principal factor in the development of Qabalah.

By what means do the planetary powers produce change in people's moods, actions, circumstances? As the ancient script has it: "As above, so below." The powers which exist in the cosmos have their focal points also in you. The directing force of Mind which operates in and beyond the cosmos is the very source of your inner being. By directing the planetary powers as they exist within your psyche—in the Deep Mind— you can achieve inner harmony, happiness, prosperity, love. You can help others. You can win your heart's desire.

The rites of Planetary Magick will powerfully open up level after level of the psyche, balancing and strengthening its perceptions and powers.
1-87542-193-8, 400 pgs., 6 x 9, color plates, softcover   19.95

GODWIN'S CABALISTIC ENCYCLOPEDIA
by David Godwin
This is the most complete correlation of Hebrew and English ideas ever offered. It is a dictionary of Cabalism arranged, with definitions, alphabetically, alphabetically in Hebrew, and numerically. With this book the practicing Cabalist or student no longer needs access to a large number of books on mysticism, magic and the occult in order to trace down the basic meanings, Hebrew spellings, and enumerations of the hundreds of terms, words, and names that are included in this book.

This book includes: all of the two-letter root words found in Biblical Hebrew, the many names of God, the Planets, the Astrological Sign Numerous Angels, the Shem Hamphorash, the Spirits of the Goetia, the Correspondences of the 32 Paths, a comparison of the Tarot and the Cabala, a guide to Hebrew Pronunciation, and a complete edition of Aleister Crowley's valuable book *Sepher Sephiroth*.

Here is a book that is a must for the shelf of all Magicians, Cabalists, Astrologers, Tarot students, Thelemites, and those with any interest at all in the spiritual aspects of our universe.
0-87542-292-6, 500 pgs., 6 × 9, softcover $15.00

FIRE & ICE
by Edred Thorsson
The hidden beliefs and practices of German occultism have long held a strong fascination for the poet as well as the historian. The greatest of the German secret lodges—the Fraternitas Saturni—revealed neither its membership, its beliefs, nor its rites. Through a chance occurrence, the inner documents of this order were recently published in Germany. *Fire & Ice* is the first study of these documents, and the inner workings of the FS which they reveal, to be published in any language.

This book relates the fascinating histories of the founders and leaders of the Fraternitas Saturni. You will witness the development of its magical beliefs and practices, its banishment by the Nazi government, and its many postwar dissensions and conflicts. The Saturnian path of initiation will be revealed in full detail, and the magical formulas which are included can be used for your own self-development as well as for more practical and concrete goals.

Fire & Ice throws a unique light on one of the world's darkest and most mysterious philosophical corners. No matter what your magical system may be, you will learn much from the adherents of *Fire & Ice!*
0-87542-776-6, 5¼ x 8, 240 pgs., illus. $9.95

A KABBALAH FOR THE MODERN WORLD
by Migene Gonzalez-Wippler
The Kabbalah is the basic form of Western mysticism, and this is an excellent manual of traditional Kabbalistic Magick! It contains one of the best introductions to the Kabbalah ever written.

If you have ever been intimidated by the Kabbalah in the past, and never studied its beauty, *this is the book for you.* It clearly and plainly explains the complexities of the Kabbalah. This is an ideal book for newcomers to the study of Kabbalah or mysticism and spirituality in general.

This book covers a variety of Kabbalistic topics including: Creation, the nature of God, the soul and soul mates, the astral and other planes, the four worlds, the history of the Kabbalah, Bible interpretation and more.

A Kabbalah for the Modern World is written so clearly that it makes complex kabbalistic ideas easy to understand. This book needs to be in the library of every occultist, Pagan, Kabbalist, mystic and person involved in the New Age.

In this book Wippler shows that the ancient Kabbalists predicted the New Physics. She goes on to discuss such topics as: Planck's Quantum Theory, God and Light, Archetypes, Synchronicity; The Collective Unconscious, the Lemaitre 'Big Bang' Theory, Einstein's Theory of Relativity and much more.

There have been many books over the past several years which have compared psychological theory and the New Age Physics with various Eastern philosophies such as Taoism and Zen. But there is only one which unites psychology, physics and *Western* mysticism: Migene Gonzalez-Wippler's *A Kabbalah for the Modern World.*
0-87542-294-2, 240 pages, 5¼ x 8, illus., softcover. $9.95

TEMPLE MAGIC
by William Gray
This important book on occultism deals specifically with problems and details you are likely to encounter in temple practice. Learn how a temple should look, how a temple should function, what a ceremonialist should wear, what physical postures best promote the ideal spiritual-mental attitude, and how magic is worked in a temple.

Temple Magic has been written specifically for the instruction and guidance of esoteric ceremonialists by someone who has spent a lifetime in spiritual service to his natural Inner Way. There are few comparable works in existence, and this book in particular deals with up-to-date techniques of constructing and using a workable temple dedicated to the furtherance of the Western Inner Tradition. In simple yet adequate language, it helps any individual understand and promote the spiritual structure of our esoteric inheritance. It is a book by a specialist for those who are intending to be specialists.

0–87542–274–8, 240 pages, 5–1/4 x 8, illus., softcover $7.95

BY STANDING STONE AND ELDER TREE
by William Gray
Originally published in 1975 as *The Rollright Ritual*, this is the re-release of this fascinating work complete with illustrations and a new introduction by the author. The famous stone circle of the "Rollrights" in Oxfordshire, England, is well known to folklorists. Gray, through the use of psychometry, has retrieved the story of the rocks from the rocks themselves—the story of the culture that placed them and the ritual system used by the ancient stone setters.

This book shows how you can create a Rollright Circle anywhere you wish, even in your own backyard, or within your own mind during meditation. Gray provides specific instructions and a script with an explanation of the language. Even for those not interested in performing the ritual, *By Standing Stone and Elder Tree* provides an exciting exploration of ancient cultures and of the value that stones hold for the fate of modern civilization.

0–87542–299–3, 208 pages, 5–1/4 x 8, illus., softcover $9.95